Praise for *Leading with Love*

There are a great many people today telling us what to think and what to do in our spiritual lives. Elaine Robinson gives us freedom from those imposed definitions by telling us why we are leaders and how to exercise that leadership. This shift in perception and action is life-giving, making her book a transformational opportunity.

—Rt. Rev. Steven Charleston, author of *We Survived the End of the World: Lessons from Native America on Apocalypse and Hope*

Robinson has written an inspiring, deeply spiritual, and eminently practical guide, not only to leadership, but to growing in the Christian spiritual life. Not just for leaders, this book will be helpful for anyone hoping to mature as a Christian. Excellent!

—Adam Hamilton, pastor and author of *Wrestling with Doubt, Finding Faith*

I wish I had *Leading with Love* as my first primer in Christian leadership when I was in my twenties. This pitch-perfect book would have become a lifelong guide for ministry. Dr. Robinson's six principles for leading with love resonate with what drew me to Christian ministry in the first place, and every page helps readers center in on what matters most—always, but especially in these challenging times. Highly recommended!

—Brian D. McLaren, author of *Faith After Doubt*

Jesus tells his disciples *not* to imitate leaders who "lord over" their subjects. Instead, they are to serve and love. But what does loving leadership look like? In this erudite but practical book, Elaine Robinson spells out how we lead in love. Few leadership books rise to the level of this one. I heartily recommend it!

—Thomas Jay Oord, author of *Pluriform Love: An Open and Relational Theology of Well-Being*

Elaine Robinson reminds us that our Christian journey is always one of growth and development as we listen deeply to God and others, learn to accept and care for ourselves physically and emotionally, and open ourselves to seeing the world through the eyes of our neighbors. Her book *Leading with Love* is a poignant reminder that these same Spirit-infused practices are also the cornerstone of authentic and effective Christian leadership. Readers will come away with a clearer understanding of how to practice authentic Christian leadership.

—F. Douglas Powe Jr., PhD, director of the Lewis Center for Church Leadership, Wesley Theological Seminary

LEADING WITH LOVE

LEADING WITH LOVE

SPIRITUAL DISCIPLINES
FOR PRACTICAL LEADERSHIP

Elaine A. Robinson

Fortress Press
Minneapolis

LEADING WITH LOVE
Spiritual Disciplines for Practical Leadership

Library of Congress Cataloging-in-Publication Data

Names: Robinson, Elaine A., author.
Title: Leading with love : spiritual disciplines for practical leadership /
   Elaine A. Robinson.
Description: Minneapolis, MN : Fortress Press, [2023] | Includes
   bibliographical references.
Identifiers: LCCN 2023012821 (print) | LCCN 2023012822 (ebook) | ISBN
   9781506488288 (print) | ISBN 9781506488295 (ebook)
Subjects: LCSH: Pastoral theology. | Christian leadership.
Classification: LCC BV4011.3 .R628 2023 (print) | LCC BV4011.3 (ebook) |
   DDC 253—dc23/eng/20230602
LC record available at https://lccn.loc.gov/2023012821
LC ebook record available at https://lccn.loc.gov/2023012822

Cover image: Wooden decorative interior finish - stock photo ©monstArrr_ |
Getty Images
Cover design: Marti Naughton

Print ISBN: 978-1-5064-8828-8
eBook ISBN: 978-1-5064-8829-5

CONTENTS

INTRODUCTION:
THE FIRST WORD IS *LOVE*

Leadership Principle One: Leadership is all about love

AT THE END of my first year as a student in the Center for Action and Contemplation's Living School, I attended a symposium in Albuquerque with other students. Richard Rohr, Brian McLaren, Barbara Holmes, and other teachers focused on the Living School as a "school for prophets," or people whose deep contemplative life led them to be agents of love and transformation in a suffering world. We were immersed in a community of likeminded people seeking to love deeply.

At the end of the second or third day, a group of us walked into Old Town to share a meal together. As the eight or nine of us gathered around a table, we quickly noticed that our waitress was stressed. "What do you want to drink?" she would snap and then return and drop the glass onto the table. "Here's your iced tea." As we began to talk about how stressed she seemed, Heidi interrupted. "Well, maybe we just need to send love her way." Then she began to say quietly, "I love you," moving her arms as if pushing that love toward the waitress on the other side of the room. Laughing, a couple of us joined in with Heidi. Whenever the woman walked away, we would sweep our arms outward toward her and repeat softly, "We love you. God loves you." It didn't take long before that waitress started smiling and softened noticeably. Did she hear us despite our attempts to be quiet about it? Was something mysterious happening in the Spirit? Whatever the case, our decision to be more loving and less judgmental changed *our* attitude. And maybe that's all it took to help dissolve her stress and tension. Love might just be the most powerful tool at our disposal as people and pastors. The first leadership principle, if we're living in the Spirit, is love. Leadership in faith communities is all about love.

But do we need a book to tell us to lead our faith communities with love? Many of us came into ministry because of our love for God and God's

people. After all, the Great Commandment is the heart of Christian discipleship. But what if we haven't really learned the meaning and fullness of living
and leading with love? What if our "love" has been formed and distorted
by the norms and structures of the Church or other cultural realities? We've
learned well how to do church and lead church, but many Christians have
never learned how to live our lives deeply in God. We might be pretty good
at leading a human institution and getting people involved in church, but
we ought to be focused on leading God's people into the depths of the spiritual life, where love is activated fully in us and through us.

Now, don't get me wrong. I appreciate my denomination, and I love
my local congregation and its people. We can't do life in the Spirit without
others, which inevitably means institutional forms and structures are necessary. But in recent years, I've also come to see how the human institution
often gets it wrong. Sometimes we learn the lessons of our church so well
that we may miss or refuse what God is doing in our midst. Or maybe we, as
pastors, see what God is doing, but motivating our people to do something
new is nearly impossible. Let's face it: This is not an easy time to be in pastoral ministry. We love God, but God's Church can be messy and difficult.

Little wonder that many pastors today are experiencing burnout.
Our current context might be the most difficult and demanding time that
church leaders have ever faced. The list of challenges is long. We've seen a
growing percentage of disaffected Americans who might be "spiritual" but
see no value in organized religion. The old ways of attracting members just
don't work. Despite surveys that demonstrate how lonely people are today,
especially younger people, they don't seem to find that sense of community
within the church. Our membership is aging and often clings to an idealized
past as the only hope for the future. Change? No way. You keep this up,
Pastor, and the only thing we'll change is you.

In recent decades, trust in institutions has been on the decline,
whether government, schools, universities, or churches and denominations,
and fewer people view institutions as promoting well-being for the larger
population. For many, institutions appear increasingly self-serving. Societal
turmoil leads to division and discord that regularly flare up within congregations, and such divisions are often fueled by social media and mass
communications.

Then add into the mix a global pandemic, which forced adaptation in ways that will become part of the landscape of ministry well into the foreseeable future. People aren't returning to the sanctuary. Online worship, among other things, is here to stay. So much is changing and uncertain. Is it any wonder ministers feel especially burned out and overwhelmed? How do we lead well in a time of division, distrust, disaffection, and uncertainty? The world is simply a more complex context than pastoral leaders have faced in the past. How do pastoral leaders manage the pace of change and equip themselves to lead during such tumultuous times? How can we help the way, the truth, and the life become incarnate in this specific context of the twenty-first century? How can we love this generation and this time in history?

A good place to begin is with those writers who suggest the church is in the midst of an every-five-hundred-year reformation. Writers such as Phyllis Tickle and Brian McLaren have long suggested that every half millennium or so, the church undergoes reform, and new shapes of faithful discipleship emerge.[1] The disruptions we experience today fit this pattern, and it is a context beyond our control. Rather than seeing this time as unfortunate or worrisome, what if we approach it as a rich opportunity to reengage the gospel and allow the Word to become flesh in this time and place? To lead into God's future, today's pastoral leaders need a different set of skills than our predecessors did, and that's what this book hopes to illuminate. We can't change the context we're in, but we can do something about our mindset and skill set.

Of course, there are skills that pastors have always needed to lead well, and those things haven't changed. For example, having a clear mission and vision, building healthy teams, attending to the culture of a congregation, and ensuring pastoral integrity remain vitally important skills.[2] Self-understanding, working through conflict, and spiritual grounding continue as much-needed capacities.[3] Certainly, addressing change and how to motivate people toward such adaptation is central to the current era of reformation and something we'll consider in chapter 5.[4] But given the context we face today, leaders need a deeper spirituality, one that rekindles ancient, even mystical, practices of the Spirit. We also need to understand the growing body of brain science around bias and emotional intelligence and the importance of intercultural competence in a global context that is experiencing constant migration. We need the capacity to understand and analyze contexts and systems, recognizing what we can change and how to do so. And we need vision that moves beyond the present and into the future that God is calling us toward. After all, the church is simply a vehicle for God's promised future breaking into the world in the present moment. It is not, itself, ever fully the way of Jesus Christ. But it should illuminate and enliven that way.

Let me throw another wrench into the works. Remember the claim that maybe we know how to do church but are lacking the formation to do life deeply in God? Too many Christians—and this includes pastors—have been taught how to do a particular form of "church" with the expectation that they will simply uphold what they have received. We learn what someone considers the "correct" teachings of the Bible or some framework of "biblical" morality, but we aren't always taught to ask questions, even though Jesus was the Questioner in Chief. Search the Gospels and look at how many times Jesus asks questions rather than answering them. We argue about whose positions on various social issues are the "right" ones, but have we learned at least to understand where they're coming from and see both sides as Jesus did? And to love the people on both those sides? You can't build a bridge unless you can see both sides of the river. We still might disagree, but at least we can respect their humanity and engage them with kindness. We create institutions and more institutions to uphold our own narrow perspectives and then justify them in God's name. At times, we act as if we know God better than anyone else, maybe better even than God.

The paradox here is that we have to open ourselves to the depths of God but in a way that dismantles or dissipates the self, the sense of "my way" as the focal point or lens through which we see the world and our faith. The depths of the spiritual life take us in a different direction from insisting our way is the right way. We learn to experience the world in a far less dualistic and rigid framework. We begin to see nuances and ambiguity. We begin to see more holistically. This is the Way. It's never fully accessible to us but becomes somewhat clearer as we allow our human lenses to soften and become more flexible. We begin to take on the mind of Christ. It's the only way that can lead to the fullness of life for everyone and everything. It leads to the fullness of love. We begin to experience a quieter, deeper ability to be present to God and others, one that is filled with love as more than simply an emotion. Love takes shape in how we live. Jacqui Lewis calls it *fierce love* and explains how it opens space in us and our world: "Fierce love causes us to cross boundaries and borders to discover one another, to support one another, to heal one another. When we do this, when we go crazy with affection, and offer wild kindness to our neighbor across the street or across the globe, we make a new kind of space between us."[5]

There is something mysterious about love. We can't fully understand love, explains Thomas Jay Oord, just as we can never fully understand God. There's an overabundance of meaning, nuance, and expression. But from what we can and do know from the Scriptures, Jesus, and our experience, "to love is to act intentionally, in relational response to God and others, to promote overall well-being."[6] As Oord summarizes, "Love wants flourishing to flourish."[7] Love is always and only found, expressed, and furthered in relationships.

Love as the heart of the gospel is nothing new or trendy. Love was central for Jesus, Paul, and the early Church. If we think the early Church was closest to Jesus's and Paul's teaching, at least in time and space, then the early Christian understanding of love can prove insightful. Roberta Bondi, in her study of the *abbas* and *ammas*, those religious men and women we might think of as monks of the early Church, makes clear that love was their guiding principle. For these Christians, who sought the depths of the Spirit and the Christian life, Jesus's command to the rich young man in Matthew 19:21 was fundamental: "If you wish to be perfect, go, sell your possessions, and give the money to the poor . . . then come, follow me." But, says Bondi, "They understood it to be another way of phrasing the Great Commandment . . . To be a perfect human being, a human being the way God intends human beings to be, is to be a fully loving person."[8] Early Christians knew that "perfect love is the goal of the Christian life."[9] But that notion wasn't legalistic. It couldn't be generated by means of law or ritual: "No amount of pious behavior or Christian discipline can replace love."[10] Nor was perfect love some instantaneous and easily obtained state. Rather, as Bondi makes clear, "Our growing love is a continuous movement into God's love, as the ancient Christian writers say. . . . This means that though we may love fully at one moment, it is not perfect love unless that love continues to grow."[11]

So often we have expectations that once we confess Jesus Christ, love of God and neighbor will be given in an instant. But Bondi says,

> Our ancestors made no such assumptions about Christian love. Gregory of Nyssa, for example, characterized the life of the monk in three stages. At the beginning, she or he serves God out of fear, like a slave; next, the service of God stems from the desire for a reward, like that of a hired hand. Only in the final stage does this person serve God out of friendship with God, or out of the pure love of God, as a child of God's household. . . . The love of God is conceived of as being difficult, something to be learned over a very long time.[12]

Love is thus an attitude, a habit, a practice, a disposition, a way of seeing and acting, a pronounced change in the heart of the believer. It takes a lifetime of practice to become the loving person we are created to be. The earliest Christians understood this. We are created for love. We are created to love. We are created to become love. To be perfect as God is perfect is simply to love deeply and fully.

Like Christians of every generation, we turn to spiritual practice as the way to learn about and grow in love. Love leads us into the world as agents of faith, hope, love, and justice. Without tapping into the depths of the spiritual life, the Church will continue to present itself, far too often, as little more than the desperate expressions of broken people trying to prove their righteousness. The Church was meant to be a place of healing and wholeness—which, at heart, is the meaning of salvation—and yet we turn love into judgment and dehumanization. Thankfully, God isn't done with us yet. We can begin to do things differently. The Church needs people willing to do the hard work of learning how to take on the mind of Christ and lead others to do the same. Then, maybe, we can love and seek justice for everyone and everything amid the suffering and messiness of life on earth.

What Is Leadership Anyway?

Let's begin by trying to define the meaning of *leadership* within the context of faith communities.[13] What are we called to do in this role? Our leadership is a spiritual practice, and we undertake it with God, and God's reconciling work in the world, at the center. We model spiritual grounding and practice, of course, but to model it, we really do need to practice it ourselves. Often. Even daily. We do a million other things, but they all flow from our spirituality, our openness to God's formative work in us. In other words, spirituality is the driving engine of our leadership. It's the well from which we draw the living water we offer to others. Thus, for anyone leading a faith community, the definitions of *leadership* used by businesses and even nonprofits are a helpful starting point, but we'll need to take another step and place God and the *missio Dei* at the center of our definition. Despite what some have claimed, church leaders aren't little CEOs of their congregations. We are light shiners; salt spreaders; table turners; feet washers; multitude feeders; and unconditional, infinite lovers.

One of the most prominent scholars of leadership, Peter Northouse, writes that "there are almost as many different definitions of *leadership* as there are people who have tried to define it."[14] Northouse demonstrates that over the past century, leadership definitions have focused on control, influence, directing groups of people, the behavior of the leader and of those led, and more recently, processes and moral responsibility. Even so, there is a common thread: "*Leadership* is a process whereby an individual influences a group of individuals to achieve a common goal."[15] In other words, leaders guide a process that encourages others to participate in moving that group of people toward a discernable, even measurable goal or outcome. It's like when I went on an Outward Bound alpine mountaineering course years ago. The experienced group leader continually moved us toward summits and campsites, using his vast knowledge and connection to those mountains in ways the rest of us hoped to learn and grow from. We were excited to follow and to experience the mountains, but we couldn't manage this journey on our own. Even so, without our commitment to the experience, his leadership wouldn't have been necessary.

For faith communities, the discernable outcome or the goal of our shared work is found in God as revealed in Jesus Christ and sustained by the Holy Spirit. Our driving logic and destination is the living God and God's love for the universe. A secular leader can and does use their best knowledge and skills. But anyone who hopes to lead God's people needs a spirituality that will enfold them and hold them together. We need a spirituality that enables us and the people to see and experience anew the depths of the living God. We need the Guide revealed in Jesus Christ and the Holy Spirit. And of course, just like that mountain guide, we need a lifetime of experiencing those depths in God to lead well. We need to step away often, as Jesus did, and sit quietly alone with God so that our own wells might be refilled. You can't overflow if the well has gone dry. You can't hear God's voice if you're too busy shouting orders or preaching at the people.

But let's continue toward a definition of *leadership* in the setting of a faith community. For Lovett Weems, it's a "ministry of stewardship . . . the proper stewardship of purpose, time, resources, opportunities, challenges, and energies of the people of God [by which] vital ministry and mission take place."[16] Drawing on Scott Cormode's work, Weems describes leadership as "a channel of God's grace" in which leaders "help God's people discern to what God is calling them and help them take that next faithful step."[17] In *Leading the Congregation*, Roger Heuser and Norman Shawchuck offer a definition focused on "*leading in order to serve for the sake of others*,"[18] which incorporates Carole Becker's notion that leadership creates community, synergy, and *something new*.[19]

Something new or the next faithful step is a good place to start for those who wish to lead a faith community. Leading a faith community means looking to the future, not only for one's own well-being or even the institution's well-being but for the whole of God's creation. Genesis 1:28 makes clear our human role as caretakers of all the earth that God has made. We are not yet fully what God promises we shall be in the new creation. We are people on a journey, trying to live here and now in God's reign (*basileia*) while awaiting its fulfillment. We are called to make visible the reign of God that has drawn near in Jesus, who is the Christ, and invite others into that new way of living as deeply relational, interconnected people who love.

For our purposes, then, we'll define *leadership* as faithful and hopeful attention to grow into God's promised future of love and justice so it draws near in a particular time and place. This practice of envisioning and enacting God's future is a form of midwifery bound up in faith, hope, and love. We help to birth something new, but really, we aren't in charge. We aren't the ones giving birth but those who are there in knowledge and love to assist. The primary Christian virtues of faith, hope, and love serve as an umbilical cord connecting us to the living God, who is birthing the new.[20] These qualities must imbue our leadership. Faith, hope, and love feed and sustain us. Though, of course, the greatest of these is always love, God's love, *agape*, for everything that exists. Everything and everyone. *Agape* is like the connective tissue or neural pathways of the universe. It holds everything together for good.

Faithful leadership is intended to birth the gospel anew in each era, culture, and context so that God's promised future may break into our world. We help to birth the gospel anew in the people gathered together under our care. We, as the body of Christ, facilitate a specific, incarnate form of being God's people. We must learn to live out of the principle of incarnation as the starting point for a reconciled and beloved new creation rather than simply getting stuck on the cross as our central symbol and immobilized in our work of futuring. More later about rebalancing the crucifixion with the meaning of the incarnation. Leadership, then, becomes a process of growing in love, helping others to grow in love, and pouring out love into a broken and suffering world. Leading with love is our calling and the single most important vocation in the universe. I suspect if you're reading this book, you want to love well, widely, and wildly. So let's turn to this thing we call *love* and take a deeper look.

Beginning the Journey of Love

Love is the signature of God and is written into the whole of creation. We live in a "Christ-soaked world," as Richard Rohr aptly articulates.[21] All of creation breathes with one breath. All of creation beats with one heart. The trees of the field clap their hands, and the mountains and hills burst into song (Isa. 55:22). We are created to experience and share the loving presence of God pulsing through everything. Rocks, trees, mountains, oceans, tulips, bok choy, ants, whales, falcons, terriers and tabbies, and each human being exactly as they have been created. In our joy and in our suffering, God is present. We are loved infinitely and unconditionally, no strings attached (though we do like to attach them to suit our perspective). Every molecule and atom pulses with the love and creative power of the living God. Our practice of faith and our leadership of faith communities are intended—in and through our love of God and neighbor—to honor and give life to all that God has deemed good.

And if God's signature is written into the whole of creation, the universe is a radically related reality. *Radical* is a word that means going to the roots or getting to the origin of a thing. At the beginning. In the beginning. God created a world that is woven together with love. Love is the glue that holds it together. We just don't see it or experience it most of the time. I'm not suggesting evil, suffering, and injustice aren't real or somehow need to be ignored. Far from it. I am suggesting we can learn to see and live into the interrelatedness of all of God's creation and set aside many of our judgments and divisions that create a lot of suffering. And then we can get to the difficult task of dealing with the depths of evil and suffering.

God loves every atom and molecule of creation in whatever form it takes, and we are to learn to love as God loves. Love is the Great Commandment Jesus gave to his followers. We are to pour out the love of God like a gushing fountain. Splash it with abandon on ourselves and everyone and everything we encounter. Salvation, at heart, doesn't mean going to heaven, though that may come after this life. The notion of heaven is shrouded in mystery, and Jesus says a lot more about how to live here and now than he does about a place called *heaven*.

Our word *salvation* comes from the Latin *salvus*, which translates as "safe, well, healthy, and saved." Add to this the Hebrew understanding of *shalom*, which English translates as "peace" but means much more than simply the absence of conflict. It means completeness, wholeness, things as they should be. When Jesus said, "Peace be with you," he meant *shalom*, healing and wholeness in the present. Salvation, then, means becoming who we are created to be and enabling the whole of God's creation to do the same. We are only "saved" when all things are allowed to exist and thrive as God intends. Here, the Indigenous understanding that all the earth is living resonates well, as every pebble, pecan tree, sage bush, surging surf, and snow-capped peak is made of the very same stuff as human beings: atoms and molecules. We are all interrelated. I once read about a scientist whose father had died, but he knew his father's molecules and atoms were now living in the birds, flowers, and trees he enjoyed as he walked in nature. The signature of God is written on every created thing.

As leaders, we are called to develop spiritual senses or sensibilities in ourselves and in our congregations, which is about, to use the phrase of Paul, taking on the mind of Christ (1 Cor. 2:16). Our love of God and neighbor, the healing and wholeness of everyone and everything (i.e., salvation), our life as it's meant to be lived are found in the deep oneness, the radical relationality of the whole of the universe as created by God. If we do not lead toward oneness, toward the reconciliation of all things, and toward love as the only sacred principle worth dying for, then our leadership will fall short of the glory of God and our calling in Jesus Christ. The most basic message of the gospel is radical relationship in and through Jesus Christ, which, paradoxically, already exists if we can learn how to inhabit it. It is finished, if we will draw near and participate. We come to realize that everything created by God is woven together for our good.

Unfortunately, we human beings like to place ourselves at the center and only love what we deem good from our narrow viewpoint. We like to judge who and what is worthy of God's love. We like to judge who and what is worthy of the church's love. We like to judge who and what is worthy of *my* love. But God's love is already present to those we exclude, and our exclusions cannot change that fact. It can only harm us and others. When we exclude, we cannot be whole or complete. Without recognizing the love that weaves the universe together and seeks flourishing for everyone, we might have a human organization that is doing well by worldly standards, *my* way might be "winning" the day, but we won't be participating in the reign of God, the kingdom of heaven, that has drawn near in Jesus Christ and is saturated with the Spirit. We won't be making the promised future inhabitable. We won't be birthing the new. We won't be agents of reconciliation.

Deep within the Christian tradition lies a way that enables us to lead amid conflict, division, and discord. The scriptural witnesses remind us that God's people have always faced times of division within and beyond the faith community. (Do you remember that the chosen people became a divided kingdom after King Solomon? Look at 1 Kings 12.) But the ministry of leadership seems particularly difficult in an age of social media and mass communication, sometimes giving misinformation that shapes and forms the hearts and minds of the people, often more powerfully than their brief engagements with the gospel. Today's proliferation of churches, each claiming to bear the truth or the true way of Jesus, can drive a wedge in the body of Christ such that our human brokenness shines more brightly than the love of God in Jesus Christ and the Holy Spirit.

There is nothing wrong with a variety of expressions of loving God and neighbor. It's when we proclaim we are the ones who have the "right" church or teachings or laws that we've lost our way and set up a system of our own making in the name of God. Failing to engage the critical questions of human existence, including destructive human systems, and focusing on "my salvation" through a "personal" savior, the Christian faith no longer draws the "nones" or "spiritual but not religious." Churches are often spiraling inward on themselves.

The phrase *my personal Lord and savior* isn't biblical but seems to have arisen in the late nineteenth century and was ingrained into Christians' consciousness by Charles Fuller in the twentieth century. As Frank Viola and George Barna explain, "The phrase *personal savior* is yet another recent innovation that grew out of the ethos of nineteenth-century American revivalism. It originated in the mid-1800s to be exact. But it grew to popular parlance by Charles Fuller (1887–1968). Fuller literally used the phrase thousands of times in his incredibly popular *Old Fashioned Revival Hour*. . . . At the time of his death, it was heard on more than 650 radio stations around the world."[22]

Jesus isn't mine, as if a personal possession we can use at will. Jesus is a communal, relational, connection point. Jesus is always, indivisibly, ours. Shared equally. How can we bring to light the relational reality of the gospel? How do we begin to move ourselves and our faith communities beyond these divisions and disconnects? How can we lead to a place of unity, harmony, reconciliation, peace, and meaningful engagement? How can our leadership point and move increasingly toward and into love? From the first century down through each generation, the answer has been found in the way taught and walked by Jesus, who is the risen Christ and who has given us the Spirit of life. If we will only pay attention.

The Way and Its Many Ways

The way of love has been taking shape since God created all that exists and first called Abraham. But for Christians, it comes to its fullest expression in

Jesus: God incarnate as a conscious, communicating, socially and culturally formed human being. The infinite God took on particular and finite flesh in Jesus. Atoms and molecules came together to form the only Jesus of Nazareth, who in his birth, life, death, and resurrection is the Christ. This particularity suggests two important things. First, the incarnation of Jesus provides our fullest, though still partial, revelation of who God is and the fullest revelation of what it means to be human as we were created to be. Fully God and fully human. Although we continue to "see in a mirror dimly" (1 Cor. 13:12),[23] Jesus discloses what we can and should know about God and our truest human nature and that the two things are connected. We can't be fully human unless we are deeply connected to God and the web of life God has created. In many ways, the atonement, the reconciliation of God and human beings, begins at the incarnation, not at the crucifixion. Jesus is fully God and fully human from the moment he is born. And in taking on human flesh, God reminds us of our basic goodness. We are worthy of God just as we are, however our flesh might look, however those atoms and molecules arrange themselves. We humbly recognize that in our finitude, we can never grasp or express the fullness of God. Yet, in the Word become flesh, we are offered a glimpse of the way, the truth, and the life to which God calls the whole of creation. Here is our map and our guide to healing and wholeness.

Second, the incarnation indicates that not all of the Bible is to be weighted equally. After all, we aren't followers of the ancient Jewish law. Jesus fulfilled the law. We are followers of Jesus, and his teachings are the standard by which we read everything else. As the fullest revelation we have, Jesus must be our bottom line. When someone proclaims we are to uphold a law in Leviticus—a teaching Jesus would have known well—we must ask ourselves: but what did Jesus teach or do? Remember, he often pushed back on the human use and misuse of the law and Scriptures. Too often, in the hands of human beings, the Bible becomes a weapon to exclude and to dehumanize rather than the Word that offers life. Jesus pointed toward the Spirit, the intention of the law, which was to give life, and we too often want to go back to the letter of the law. We want control. We want our privilege and power intact at the expense of "those ungodly people." We want to nail down God, but God always rises to overcome and take down our tendency to remake the Word in our own image. The incarnation of God in Jesus helps us to see who God is and who we should be. It helps us learn to read the Bible with Christ at the center and the margins as our guide for understanding. It helps us to see that God will become who God will become (Exod. 3:14), and it's not up to us to place boundaries around whom God chooses to love. Which is everyone. And everything.

To push this conversation one step further, because God will be who God will be, the way of Jesus isn't a destination. It's not a momentary confession. It's a process or a journey. The way is a path we walk and help others to travel. The way is a process of learning to love, to see, and to do as God loves, sees, and does. It unfolds in the going. Too many Christians want clarity or answers before making a decision, but that's certainty, not faith. Faith steps out into a mist or a fog that envelops the way. Besides, much of the time there isn't one way to proceed but several faithful options. I tell my students that God is a bit like Yogi Berra, who famously declared, "When you come to a fork in the road, take it."

Have you ever noticed that in the Scriptures, many profound encounters with God take place after Moses or Elijah or the disciples have climbed up a mountain? The spiritual giant Saint John of the Cross understood that mountains are a perfect metaphor for the faith journey. We are called to climb higher day by day. As if hiking up a mountain, sometimes we step off the trail, whether intentionally or simply because we lose sight of the path. Or we grow weary, stumble, or become distracted. And as we go, the path leads us to a different place and a different way of seeing the world and ourselves. We can't see the valley stretching below unless we keep climbing. We can't see the stark beauty of the summit unless we keep climbing. As we walk the path, we see and experience new things, even on a trail we've hiked many times before. A friend and I once came on some beautiful lavender fungi on a trail he's hiked hundreds of times and had never seen before or since. We can't climb the mountain without the steps we've already taken, but those previous steps are never enough to reach the summit. There are no shortcuts to the summit, but we walk trusting that something beautiful and soul-stirring lies ahead. That's faith in following Jesus.

There is yet a second thing about Jesus's way that we need to wrestle with: the way has many paths we can travel. Of course, there is one incarnate Jesus of Nazareth, who is the risen Christ. But there are so many expressions of faith in Jesus bearing faithful witness across the earth. Remember that each of us is created as a specific human being in a particular time and place. We have diverse gifts and varying experiences of life. No one else will ever live my unique existence. Each of us will experience life and our faith in unique contexts and experiences.

Then, in all our uniqueness, we come together as the body of Christ and form one unrepeatable, irreplaceable faith community. Jesus gave no blueprints for the *ekklesia,* or those he calls together out of the world. He didn't give us any rules or regulations except to remind us that it's all about love (Matt. 22:37–39; Mark 12:30–31; Luke 10:27)—and to insist we take the log out of our own eye before pointing to the splinter in someone else's (Matt. 7:3; Luke 6:41). Whether we admit it or not, we all have quite a few logs narrowing our perspective. Sometimes we are so used to the log that we don't even realize it's there. Jesus's way is simply about learning to love and getting rid of a lot of stuff that keeps us from doing that well.

Love God with everything you are and love your neighbor as you love yourself. That's the one thing Jesus tells us to get right. The meaning of love might be the most important question we ever ask ourselves as followers of Jesus. This is God's own *agape* love, the love that exists among the divine community, those three "persons" of the Trinity. We will never fully grasp this infinite love. Often, we equate love with feeling, and there can be an affective, emotional component to love. But we are to love whether we feel love or not. Love is best revealed in the way we live in community. Love has the power to heal and make whole. Perhaps *only* love has the power to heal and make whole.

I've heard some Christians demand that love must first have a moral component, or it's not godly love. But the problem, of course, is they usually mean their own moral standards, held up as if perfectly aligned with God's expectations. As we'll argue in later chapters, love will lead us to live good lives, ethical lives, but starting with the law or rules will never teach us to love. All human beings fall short of God. God doesn't measure sins as greater or lesser, the way we like to do. And all are loved by God. All.

I'm also pretty sure God's view of sin differs from ours, if God even cares about what we condemn as *sin* since we seem to get this wrong over and over again. We often use sin as a means, a justification to exclude those we don't like or who are different from us or make us uncomfortable. The only unpardonable sin is "blasphemy against the Spirit," or maybe against love, per Matthew 12:31. It suggests setting ourselves up as God and telling others they aren't lovable or worthy of God in their sinful state. It rejects what the Spirit is doing. The Spirit is divine love arcing outward from that trinitarian dance and splashing down onto the world that God so loves, on everyone and everything. The Spirit gathers and unites in a bond of love. At heart, sin should be understood as our failure to love someone or something in the way God loves. Sin thwarts God's life-giving goodness and breaks the radical relationships that God has created and sustains. Blasphemy against the Spirit is nothing less than rejecting that God's love is unconditional, infinite, everywhere, and for everyone. But even the best of us, the most accepting of the widely and wildly open arms of *agape*, fail to love at times; that's our human dilemma.

Although the incarnation is often quickly passed over in the story of Jesus, its message is essential to shaping our practice of love. Do you ever preach about the incarnation beyond Advent and Christmas? Or, on Epiphany, do you tuck it away in the attic with the nativity scene, the evergreen branches, and the "Silent Night" candles? Christmas Eve is so beloved because of the depths of the message of God's pure love. We proclaim the baby born in the manger as the Savior of all. Then we jump to a grown-up Jesus teaching us what we need to know. Talking to our minds. But first he spoke simply to our hearts. The newborn baby reveals God's way to us: infinite, unconditional love poured into a real human being and given to all.

If we don't get the message of the incarnation right, we'll have a hard time getting the rest of the story right. If we insist and focus on the cross as the center of the faith rather than an equal partner in the God story, we narrow our sight to focus on sin and judgment and, indeed, death rather than life. We keep pointing out how other people (not me) are crucifying Jesus with their ungodly ways. The cross is a place where we stand our ground firmly; it's not where we best follow Jesus into the uncertainty of faith, hope, and love. The crucifixion is a stark reminder not only of what Jesus has done for us but also what we have done and continue to do to him. When we don't embrace the whole story and refuse to hear and live all his teachings, we tend to reject his message just as some religious people did two thousand years ago. But Jesus willingly and humbly suffers our slings and arrows as an expression of unconditional, infinite love. Rebalancing the crucifixion with the incarnation, ministry, and resurrection of Jesus is a needed corrective in the twenty-first century.

Here, let's add two insights given to us in the incarnation. First, God didn't have to come to us as an infant. As in the Gospel of Mark, Jesus could have walked out of the wilderness, fully grown, and started teaching, healing, and performing miracles. But the story we tell every Advent and Christmas (and now, hopefully, at other times of the year) begins with a helpless, vulnerable baby. Long before God announces that "this is my body given for you" at the crucifixion, God says in the incarnation, "This is my body, given for you. Love me. Care for me. Nurture this gift." It is a sign of God's unconditional love as babies don't make the distinctions we do. No sin. No judgment. No expectations. Just pure love. Second, a baby can't survive without relationships. The child needs a community in order to survive and thrive. There's an inescapable message of relationship, a message of not being able to go it alone if we hope to survive and thrive. We are intended to care for each other, to feed and clothe and tenderly hold one another, to live as if our very lives depend on our relationships. And they do.

Brain science now suggests that if a child isn't held and nurtured in the first few months of life, they will experience ongoing trauma and difficulties forming and maintaining relationships, a point to which we'll return in chapter 3.[24] Take hold of the message of the incarnation: we are in this thing called *life* together, and we only survive and thrive when we are in relationships of caring, nurture, and love. How often do we miss this message? Simply put, the starting point for Jesus's way is 1) God's infinite and unconditional love, and 2) the fact that we are born into relationships, and those relationships are intended to be life-giving and life-furthering. The story of Jesus begins here and shapes the whole of the gospel.

No one knows exactly how the atonement (the *at-one*-ment, or reconciliation of God and humanity) takes place, and every seminary student knows there have been multiple theories of atonement throughout Christian history. Maybe none of them is right. Maybe a bit of each one is right. We don't really know how this mystery works, even though we might argue for a particular theory as the one we've been taught to believe. As we've noted above, in the incarnation, God and humanity are already reconciled, an insight articulated by Athanasius in the early Church (yes, one of those theories). Each moment in the life of Jesus bears equal and important significance for the life of faith, but we don't wear a manger or an empty tomb around our necks. We wear the cross, which was an instrument of death, not life. Without the incarnation and the resurrection, there is only a dead would-be messiah who maybe wasn't even fully divine but only appeared to be. The proclamation of life and love at the beginning and end of Jesus's story is what holds the pain of the cross together. The cross reminds us that Jesus shares in our suffering, not simply that he "died for my sins."

The message of the cross isn't just Jesus's forgiveness and presence in our suffering, but it also reveals our unwillingness to accept his message of love and life and our need to turn God's gift into judgment and death. God didn't send Jesus to the cross; we did. The law is used to crucify Jesus. Religious and political systems crucify Jesus. We demand death because we want to be right and insist on our own way more than we want to love and give life to others. We want to eliminate any message that threatens our beliefs and practices. We'd rather use our power and privilege to do harm than to lay down those things in exchange for giving life to others. And still we haven't learned the lesson of the cross. We need to stop killing love and one another in myriad ways. Love can't be self-centered or my-people-centered or even my-institution-centered. Love is given to all so that we might have life and abundance.

If salvation is about healing and wholeness, then we are called to be agents of that healing and wholeness in the world. Givers of life. We, ourselves, each of us and all of us, first need to open ourselves to that healing process given by the grace of God. This is loving ourselves. When we love God enough to surrender our ego-driven demands and desires (i.e., work at getting out those logs), we then allow the Christ character to take up its home in us and work through us for the healing of the world. Love is healing. Love is life-giving. Love is patient, kind, long-suffering. It doesn't insist on its own way (1 Cor. 13: 4–8). We aren't going to love just because we say we love. In fact, too many churches "love everyone" with their words, but their actions—often without their awareness—suggest otherwise. Leaders need to grow in love, and they need to help their faith communities grow in love. Again, if we get this wrong, we aren't following Jesus. We may be a church, but we fall short of the love poured into Jesus.

Every generation struggles to remain open to the way God stretches out before us. Every generation seems intent on clinging to the way "it used to be." But human beings aren't designed to live backward in time. We aren't created to remain unchanged through our lives or through the centuries. We are created to grow. The way of love has never been about a strict set of rules and regulations or the adherence to a set of beliefs and moral codes that are unchanging in their meaning and application.[25] We certainly don't follow the laws of ancient Israel. We don't even follow the same laws that existed one or two hundred years ago. We find blue laws laughable. We should condemn any reinvention of legalized slavery or Jim Crow laws. Boarding schools for Native peoples are an evil that must never again exist. Allowing women to only become teachers or nurses should sound ridiculous. Would we, today, tell someone with eczema they're unclean and must isolate from the rest of the community? We've learned something since then that climbs a little closer to the summit of God's way. But we aren't there yet.

Jesus's way was never intended to be a momentary confession that enables us to sit back on our haunches and wait for an express train to heaven's gate. The way has always been a process, an intentional journey, a daily choice in which we are to grow in love and compassion, not only for those who share our views and cultural norms but for each and every atom and molecule in the universe. We are called to become love. Learning to see as Jesus sees, to take on the mind of Christ, can enable us to live and love as Jesus did in our own time and place. Only then can we lead others into the depths of love and compassion. Compassion, healing, giving hope, laying down our own demands—these things are the way we express the love that is given in Jesus Christ. It is the only way to salvation, to the gift of healing and wholeness for everyone and everything. In many ways, salvation is only realized when the whole of creation is restored. My "personal" salvation will never fulfill the restoration that God promises. We are in this together with each other and all of God's creation, or we aren't really following Jesus at all.

The chapters ahead present a leadership model rooted and grounded in love. It is a way that can never be fully understood, grasped, or lived as finite creatures but must be pursued with passion every day. We are invited to take on the mind of Christ, to let go of the egocentric perspective and the dualisms it creates and perpetuates, and to embrace the unified way of love that Jesus lived and calls us to embody in words and actions. God needs leaders who seek to be love rather than to be right, and love embodies humility and compassion. It requires prayer and practice. It demands growth and change. Love is meant to become incarnate in our world over and over again.

We might go so far as to suggest that Jesus Christ should return in each generation alive and incarnate in us and through us. Waiting for Christ to return? Perhaps Christ is waiting for us to incarnate the way, right where we are and as we are. Love must become flesh here and now. Whenever and wherever love is given and received, Jesus Christ is present, and the reign of God draws near. Whether we are leading the faith community or are one of the faithful who serves primarily in the world, Jesus's way invites us to grow into the depths of love. Leadership is all about love.

Practice Makes (More but Not Completely) Perfect

1. To begin, ask yourself: How well am I loving myself, others, creation, and God? Where does your ego or woundedness seem to get in the way? Where and why is it hard to live a life of love?
2. How would you describe the love expressed in your faith community? And where does it seem to break down? Are there certain groups of people or certain situations when your faith community is more likely to respond with judgment than love?
3. How might the theology or practices you've learned get in the way of your ability to love everyone and everything?

Resources for Going Deeper

Bondi, Roberta C. *To Love as God Loves: Conversations with the Early Church.* Philadelphia: Fortress Press, 1987.

Lewis, Jacqui. *Fierce Love.* New York: Harmony Books, 2021.

———. *Love Period.* Podcast series. Albuquerque: Center for Action and Contemplation. https://cac.org/podcast/love-period/.

Oord, Thomas Jay. *Open and Relational Theology: An Introduction to Life-Changing Ideas.* Grassmere, ID: SacraSage Press, 2021. (Oord's intention is to develop a reasoned and experientially valid theology of love.)

———. *Pluriform Love.* Grassmere, ID: SacraSage Press, 2022.

Rohr, Richard. *Eager to Love: The Alternative Way of Francis of Assisi.* Cincinnati: Franciscan Media, 2014.

———. *Everything Belongs: The Gift of Contemplative Prayer.* New York: Crossroad Publishing, 2003.

GROWING

Leadership Principle Two: We are designed to grow, learn, and change

WHEN I WAS young, I had a Kodak instamatic camera. It was anything but "instamatic." It required film inserted through the back. All twenty-four or thirty-six images had to be snapped before I could remove the film and take it to the store to be developed. A week or so later, my pictures were ready for pickup, but often I only received twenty-two or thirty-five because some negatives were blurred, or there was a picture of my thumb. Then, somewhere in my forties, the mobile phone emerged, and before long, cameras and film were pretty much obsolete. Kodak had to reinvent itself to stave off bankruptcy and closure. Today my photos are truly instamatic digital images ready to download and print immediately. The world of photography has, we might say, developed. And we aren't going back.

Human beings grow as individuals and as a collective or species. Things we knew and did fifty years ago—let alone two thousand—have been rethought, deepened, supplanted. What I knew and experienced as a child or young adult isn't how I live my life today. Thank goodness. Every living thing grows and changes. Every human community grows, changes, and learns new things. In fact, we might say God has designed the created world with perpetual change built in, both physically and intellectually. I don't know about you, but my faith community needs to hear this statement often. We are designed to be refined over time. To be human is to grow and change, even if—or especially if—we are following Jesus. Do you know that the basic meaning of *disciple* is "learner"? To be a follower is first to be a learner. There is always something new to discover in life, in the Scriptures, and in the mystery of the triune God.

Our second leadership principle recognizes the fundamental importance of change and growth. We are designed by God to learn, grow, and change. We can't be who God calls us to be without growing. Our minds have to be open to see and do new things across our lifetime and across human history. Likewise, our faith communities can't love well without learning and growing. We have to take our intellect seriously if we are to grow in love. Doesn't it seem strange, then, that everything grows except, at times, people who desperately want things to stay "the way we've always done it" or argue vehemently for holding on to the things they learned as children? In this chapter, we want to get our minds around the way our minds work. We are challenged to lead ourselves and our people in a developmental process that allows us to become who God has created us to be in this time and place. Remember, the Word always becomes incarnate in just this moment.

Jesus Grew in Wisdom and in Years

Let's begin again with Jesus. Luke 2:52 reminds us that "Jesus increased in wisdom and in years, and in divine and human favor." After the incarnation and those infancy narratives in the Bible, we get that fascinating glimpse of Jesus at the age of twelve. The community has traveled to Jerusalem for the festival of Passover, and as with most tribal people, they would all assume responsibility for the children. Jesus's parents aren't neglectful; they have different cultural standards at work. But then, to their horror and dismay, after a day's travel, they find he's not among the travelers at all. It takes another three days to find him! When they do, he's in the temple at the feet of the rabbis, asking questions and learning. If Jesus is compelled to study and go deeper (which his parents didn't ask him to do in this instance), it tells us something important. We don't see him again until he begins his ministry at the age of thirty, which, by the way, is the age when the human brain reaches full maturity. The earliest maturing of the brain seems to be at age twenty-five. What is Jesus doing between the ages of twelve and thirty? Learning and growing. If it takes Jesus some eighteen to thirty years to prepare for ministry, then most of us will need a lifetime to come close to his wisdom.

We know that Jesus studies the Hebrew Scriptures and will be called *rabbi* or *teacher* during his ministry. But as a human being, he also goes through the normal developmental stages. He had to learn to walk and talk, read and write. His parents had to teach him right from wrong and the rituals of Judaism. He probably learned carpentry from his father. No doubt he was taught how to be a functioning member of the community in which he lived, upholding its expectations for living together. Sometimes we think Jesus showed up fully formed, but that glimpse of him at the age of twelve reminds us that every living thing grows, develops, and changes. Again, growth and change are basic principles rooted in God's creation.

Before Jesus could be fully who he was created to be, he studied, grew, and developed over time. We understand, of course, that much of this growth is what we'd call *intellectual development*. Even Jesus's brain underwent normal human growth. Jesus wasn't born with the full understanding of the Torah poured into his tiny infant brain, even though he is fully God. That mystery of Jesus as fully God and fully human isn't meant to be solved like a riddle. It's meant to draw us into the mystery of God with wonder and awe, to show us that to be fully human requires us to be deeply connected to God and others. And it's meant to reveal to us the things God values and expects of human beings. We might say that Jesus of Nazareth grew into "the mind of Christ." This phrase, *the mind of Christ*, found in Paul's first letter to the Corinthians, is an expression we'll use throughout this book to convey a deeper and fuller way of seeing and living, a way that takes on something of a God's-eye view of everything, less dualistic and more wholistic. The mind of Christ sees things as they really are rather than "in a mirror, dimly" (1 Cor. 13:12). The mind of Christ sees the interconnectedness, the radical relationships that exist within the world God has created, redeemed, and sustained.

The mind of Christ reveals to us how to love God, others, and the whole of creation as we are called and created to love. But as Paul shows us, we don't have the mind of Christ magically poured into our brains when we choose to confess or follow Jesus Christ. Typically, we open ourselves to God's wisdom, and then we close ourselves off again. Two steps forward and one step back. Without staying open to God's Spirit, where it might lead us and what it might show us, we can't grow and learn those things that matter ultimately. Taking on the mind of Christ depends on a lifetime process of spiritual discipline and learning to let go of our ego-driven expectations in order that we, too, might grow in wisdom and in years. We will always grow in years. But will we choose to grow in wisdom?

The Mind of Christ

Let's dive into the meaning of this Pauline phrase *the mind of Christ* since it's an essential concept throughout this book. Paul's first letter to the Corinthians is a fascinating study of church divisions, and Paul considers any actions that break the unity of the body of Christ to be unspiritual and immature. When Paul tells the Corinthians, "But we have the mind of Christ" (1 Cor. 2:16), we tend to assume he means that followers of Jesus are given wisdom, and those who don't know Jesus are lacking understanding. In other words, Christians have it; non-Christians don't. But Paul's phrase is considerably more complex and, in this context, points to *Christians* who don't have the mind of Christ. To get at the meaning of the phrase, we need to study his letter from a larger perspective. It's always precarious to read a verse or two without the bigger picture, especially given the "occasional" or contextual nature of Paul's letters.

As noted above, there are some serious issues in the church at Corinth. As a major seaport, the city is a bubbling cauldron of cultural and religious diversity. A lot of different ways of living are swirling around, and those early Christians aren't immune to the pull and sway of these cultural expressions. Chapters five through eleven of Paul's letter contain a litany of moral failings that require attention, but, significantly, Paul begins with the issue of greatest concern: divisions among Christians.

Paul's church is riddled with rivalries, factions, or dissensions (the Greek word here is *schismata*, from which we get the word *schism*). Paul's purpose in writing "is clearly to bring order and unity in the Corinthian community."[1] They are arguing with each other about whose leadership to follow (1 Cor. 1:10–17). Whose way, whose practices, whose teachings, whose expectations are the "right" ones? Paul, of course, will simply remind them that they follow only Jesus and him crucified (2:2). We now encounter the central meaning of the cross as something of a unifying reality, despite, or because of, the brokenness and divisions created by human demands and desires, even among Christians, not just those who don't know God. If Jesus doesn't break the power of our human *schismata*, we'll never be one body in Christ.

The cross of Jesus Christ is a primary symbol of unity: Think of the way its vertical beam and horizontal beam are pulled together, reflecting

Jesus as mediator of the reconciliation of all things. Heaven and earth, God and human beings. All of God's creation. United and made whole. Reconciled. The cross says: You are forgiven all the ways you put yourself first at the expense of others. You are forgiven your tendency to prefer your own way and to draw lines in the sand that exclude others, call them unworthy, and break relationships. All the lines we draw are pulled back together in the cross. There is no way to healing and wholeness, salvation, without being pulled into this reconciliation in and through Jesus. The cross puts to death division and disunity.

For Paul, the message of the crucifixion is crucial to taking on the mind of Christ. Paul's premodern perspective would have held a communal sensibility over the individual, understanding that Christ died for *all*, not for "me." We might credit the Reformation, and especially Martin Luther, with helping to give the personal twist to Paul's claim—and as we'll see later, modernity goes all in with the individual focus that leads us to reject the relational meaning of the cross and make an idol out of "me." What's more, if it's about "me" and "my sins," then it's not about reconciliation at all but simply another way to put myself, rather than God, first. In that *all* is a claim as to the inescapably relational nature of being in Christ, which means factions and divisions in the body of Christ are inconsistent with the message of the cross.

Paul's leadership is about unity and reconciliation, despite differences in how we think about and see things. We all see in part. And unless we learn to see together, united in the cross that overcomes our selfishness and need to uphold "my" own way, we'll continue to fall short. Paul doesn't say, "You have the mind of Christ" or "I have the mind of Christ." He says, "*We* have the mind of Christ." It's all about that *we*. Jesus died to overcome our divisions and brokenness. Jesus died to overcome our ways of comparing who's better and who's worse, who's in and who's out, who's right and who's wrong. The cross announces, "There is no longer Jew or Greek, there is no longer slave or free, there is no longer male nor female; for all of you are one in Christ Jesus" (Gal. 3:28). The mind of Christ brings us together as one people beloved of God. *All* of us are sinful, and *all* of us are reconciled in and through Jesus Christ. That is a message of unconditional, infinite love.

When we return to Paul's letter to the people at Corinth, he builds his case in pieces, through the unfolding of the meaning of the cross. Paul tells them the cross is foolishness to many because it utterly upends worldly ways of thinking. To those who buy into the world's claims, the powerful and privileged should dictate to everyone else. The world always promotes a hierarchical pecking order in which the "stronger" get to be in charge. In the first century, people would have been taught that their station in life was God-given, and they needed to accept it. If you're rich and powerful, that's the way God wants it to be. It's the sin of comparisons: I'm better than you. As we'll see throughout this book, the sin of comparisons is a primary human failing that leads to binary, dualistic mindsets.

When the ancient people expect a messiah like King David, a great political and military leader, they are looking for the strongest of the strong to exercise his power over others. Might makes right, says the world. Don't we sometimes do the same? We want a messiah who gives us power over others through force and control. We want a young, tall, strong man to lead our congregation because that's what power looks like. We want a king, just like all the other people who don't know God. We want our way to win the day. We want our church to be the biggest and the best. See how great we are? But that's not the way of love. The message of the cross, Paul insists, is that "God's weakness is stronger than human strength" (1 Cor 1:25) and "God chose what is low and despised in the world . . . so that no one might boast in the presence of God" (1:28–29). The cross reveals that operating according to human notions of power, even in the name of God, is not the way of love. Trying to convince others that I have the way, the truth, and the life is consistent with the world, not Jesus, who never felt compelled to prove himself. He just kept gently sharing his message and healing people until those in power were so threatened that they had to get rid of him. Power over is not the way of Jesus Christ. Let go of your need to be right, to be "a number one, top of the list, king of the hill."[2] Jesus shows us the way.

In fact, Paul reiterates this point in chapter 12 when he emphasizes that no spiritual gift is better or more important than another. Those who were dividing the body of Christ were claiming to be more spiritual, holier, or godlier than Paul or others. But again, these comparisons simply demonstrate that we are not of the Spirit but quite worldly. Paul says instead that the person who takes out the trash for the community is every bit as important and valuable as the one who preaches on Sunday. We need every person and every gift of the Spirit related and interconnected to be healed and whole. Joseph Fitzmyer explains, "The many members of the Christian community must use all their diverse manifestations of the Spirit 'to the good' (12:7) of the whole, because Christ is the unifying principle of the church."[3] The body of Christ in the world is only whole through each gift and each person or part working in harmony with the others. The cross proclaims: we are all in this together, guided by Jesus's way of loving, or we are still living by our ego and turned in on ourselves.

This message is reiterated in Paul's hymn in Philippians. Paul introduces the meaning of the cross with the words, "Let the same mind be in you that was in Christ Jesus" (Phil. 2:5), which means "looking not to your own interests, but to the interests of others" (Phil. 2:4). And what does that "same mind" look like? It "did not regard equality with God as something to be exploited" (Phil. 2:6). In other words, the mind of Christ is never trying to get the upper hand or prove that my way is better. Love never operates through power over others or control. Instead of exercising that kind of power, Jesus "emptied himself," "humbled himself," "became obedient to the point of death" (Phil. 2:7–8). Jesus doesn't demand that we follow his way. God will never force our hand or heart. And if we choose to follow, then we must empty out the selfishness from "my" heart that wants to be first, better, stronger, right, or in control. The sin of comparisons leads us down the wrong path. The mind of Christ recognizes that divisions and factions are always about "my way" over "your way" but never about Jesus's unifying way of love. We are in this together, says the cross, even if you argue otherwise. Dividing, "othering" certain people, or demanding our way is the "right" way only show us that we aren't following Jesus's teaching no matter how loudly we proclaim it.

Once Paul shows the Corinthians they're still thinking just like the world and not through the message of the cross, he explains the difference between being "spiritual" (*pneumatikos*) and "unspiritual" (*psychikos*). Again, he's suggesting here that some who claim to follow Christ aren't spiritual at all but still thinking like the world, unspiritually. Someone who is a "Spirit person" is humble, empties out their ego, and becomes open to the leading of the Spirit, which blows where it may. Spirit people surrender the need to control so that they can hear and follow God's leading. Spirit people can discern and act out of love and wisdom because they've emptied out the teachings of a competitive—and for our day and age, consumeristic—mindset.

On the other hand, *psychikos*, which is difficult to translate, suggests that what activates the unspiritual person is *anima*, or human desires that block "the ability to be open to revelation or wisdom that comes from God's Spirit."[4] Think of the English word *animus*, which usually means "a spiteful or bad disposition." That person in the community who is always negative and trying to tear things down or disrupt anything that doesn't suit them personally. *Animus* can also mean the motivation to do something. Together, these definitions point us toward being wrongly motivated by personal desires as the heart is turned in on itself rather than open to receive the love of the Spirit that pulls us into a relationship with God and others. Saying it's *of God* doesn't make it so. Animus separates as it compels us to defend and preserve my way. So animus, or worldly and self-centered desire, doesn't just apply to non-Christians but to "two different types of Christians."[5] Saying I'm a follower of Jesus does not make me spiritual. Unless I stop making an idol of myself and my way, I won't be able to receive the Spirit, listen to God, and follow Jesus where he asks the faith community to go.

Paul's point is that if we are still "animated" by the motives of the world, we aren't living according to the Spirit, and we'll not have the mind of Christ, which alone gives the wisdom of God. Only through the mind of Christ do we see that reconciliation is our calling and our destination and that being together is infinitely better than where we end up when human beings demand we follow them into divisions. Those who crucified Jesus rejected the truth, love, and wisdom of God in the name of their rules, laws, and ways of holding and exercising power. Divisions demonstrate that we are still rejecting the truth, love, and wisdom of God. Only in the unity of the cross do we open ourselves to God's Spirit and set aside our animus. If we seek to divide the body of Christ, says Paul, we simply aren't open to receive God's Spirit. We aren't living out of the message of the cross.

God's wisdom is revealed in the cross, and it's a way of bringing everything together rather than pulling things apart. Dualistic thinking, then, has no place within the mind of Christ. The mind of Christ sees the radical relationships that exist throughout God's creation and embraces them as our calling and our hope. No judgment is right judgment apart from this unified perspective, and once we have the mind of Christ (the unified perspective), we no longer judge with the divisive mind of the world that categorizes some as "worthy" and others as "unworthy." The mind of Christ is the way of love. It brings us together and leads to the flourishing of all things. Love is "the more excellent way" (1 Cor 12:31). We can't fully inhabit the mind of Christ in this life as we will always see in part as finite human beings. But we can grow, if we are intentional, into a more wholistic and unified way of seeing the world through the eyes of Christ, a way that's deeply connected to the Spirit as it pours out God's love.

While some have argued that 1 Corinthians 13, Paul's discourse on love, is misplaced or a digression within this letter, Fitzmyer claims it's "the *climax* to what Paul has been teaching in chap. 12 about the *pneumatika* [spiritual gifts] and the diverse kinds of them. . . . Love is different from those endowments of the Spirit, surpassing all of them as the greatest gift of God."[6] Indeed, "these verses sum up what Paul has been saying elsewhere in this letter about the characteristics of Christian life when lived in Christ."[7] As we suggested in our introduction, leadership in faith communities is all about love. Here we need to be clear that love isn't being presented by Paul as a comparison of "better than." It's not even a superlative: the best. He's simply indicating that among all those gifts of the Spirit present in the Christian life, only love is given to everyone, only love can unite us, and only love lasts.

Love is the unifying principle. Faith becomes sight. Hope becomes fulfillment. Gifts become unnecessary. Love alone remains as the fullness or culmination of a life well lived. The Greek word that we tend to translate as love never "fails" literally means never "falls."[8] Love never falls short of God's way. Connected to God's gift in Jesus Christ, we are reconciled, glued together, one body with one baptism. In love, we find mutuality, kindness, compassion, and wholeness. The only thing that can save us is love. What a gift given to people who often want to fight, argue, be right, or walk away from "those people." The love of God in Jesus Christ and the Holy Spirit is intended to be poured into the world through us so that all of God's creation might be healed and made whole.

The mind of Christ is about seeing things with a God's-eye view, unified, as things are meant to be. The Greek word for "mind," *nous*, points to the intellect, to our thinking brain. Get your head on straight, says Paul. As we'll see in later chapters, our thinking brain is always the last part of our brain to engage, which means if we don't learn to love first, our thinking will never get us to the fullness of Christ. If we try to require beliefs or morality as the basis for love, we have it backward because the mind will always first engage in either loving relationships or animus and division. If love and healthy, life-giving relationships aren't present, we'll only fall into the trap of seeking salvation by fulfilling the law. Pour out love first in spite of people's intellectual and moral failures—just like Jesus did on the cross—and salvation has a real chance. We'll always misunderstand the cross without seeing it first as love and as a unifying reality. Our hatred and animus are transformed into love, and our brokenness and separation become unity. Such divine foolishness!

In the next chapter, we'll explore how to stop our incessant thinking long enough to listen for the wisdom of God to break into our animated (*psychikos*) lives, those subtle dualistic ways of the world. To live by the Spirit (*pneumatikos*), we must cultivate the spiritual life. Of course, thinking and reasoning aren't things to reject in favor of "having faith." Faith is about trust in God, not denying our God-given brains. These things are not opposed. After all, the mind of Christ is a way of thinking and reasoning and judging things in their unity and wholeness. Let's take a look at the impressive gift of the human brain that God has given us and how our thinking can deepen our connection to the way of love.

The Human Brain Is Fearfully and Wonderfully Made

The more we learn about the human brain, the more awe-inspiring it becomes, even though it continues to be shrouded in mysteries. Bill Bryson asserts, "The most extraordinary thing in the universe is inside your head."[9] Among all of God's creations, the brain might just be the most spectacular. Bryson explains that "sitting quietly, doing nothing at all, your brain churns through more information in thirty seconds than the Hubble Space Telescope has processed in thirty years."[10] A piece of the cortex no larger than a grain of sand "could hold two thousand terabytes of information, enough to store all the movies ever made, trailers included."[11] The function we call *intellect* occurs through the interweaving of our neural pathways, "trillions and trillions of connections."[12] In some ways, our brain is a radically related universe unto itself. It reflects the very nature of God's creation as inescapably interconnected.

Clearly, the gift of the human brain is intended to be used well. We are designed to learn. But Bryson is also clear that "there is a huge amount we [as a species] have left to learn and many things we may never learn."[13] Therein lies our call to humility. If we can't even fully understand the brain within our head, how can we possibly understand the fullness of the mysteries of God? Yet how can we not use this glorious brain to the fullest extent possible? Anything less would seem to dishonor the gift God has given us.

As a follower of Jesus, I have a hard time understanding those who promote anti-intellectualism as God's way. Jesus was anything but anti-intellectual. In fact, as we discussed above, he learned the Jewish law over many years. Perhaps he only learned from his parents. Perhaps he studied more formally in those "lost years." In any case, Jesus was a teacher, and teaching is always about getting the brain to think and then to think some more. Perhaps Jesus knew how the human brain works. Here's what I mean. Never does Jesus say, "God said it; I believe it. That settles it," as some Christians do. And what they mean is "I know what the Bible says literally and will follow it by faith." When they make this claim, they tend to close themselves off from learning and growing. But Jesus is seldom, if ever, literal.

To read something in a literal sense suggests we get to the clear, exact, "right" meaning that is intended by the author or writer. To know with certainty the true meaning as God intends. But how can faith know with certainty? How can we, as finite people, know and understand everything God reveals, especially when Jesus always speaks in parables, stories, and questions? Isn't faith about following the way of Jesus even when we don't know where we are headed? The problems we encounter when claiming to read the Bible *literally* are many, given the meaning of the word. These problems are worth pondering as they demonstrate that being literal is more about holding an unchanging position than getting deeper into a truer understanding of God's way in Jesus Christ.

First, there are very few Christians who know biblical Hebrew and Koine Greek well. Paying attention to footnotes in our translations, we often encounter "meaning of the Hebrew word uncertain." So a translation is never as literal as one might claim. That's why there are the multitude of different translations and some paraphrases that take liberties with the original text to help the meaning, as understood by the translator, become clearer. Second, even those who know the biblical languages well don't live in the premodern mindset or the culture of the first century, and language always has nuances according to the culture in which we live. In the eighteenth century, *awful* meant "awe-filled." But if someone leaving the sanctuary tells you your sermon was awful today, you aren't likely to thank them. But the third problem for reading in a literal sense is revealed in Jesus's method of teaching and explaining the mysteries of God. He uses metaphors, stories, analogies, and parables. These forms of speech are intended *not* to be taken literally. They seek to draw us in, make us think, and then encourage us to think some more. Don't assume, says Jesus, that you know what the reign of God is like. You need to learn more about it. You haven't mastered this yet. There's more I want you to see.

Jesus teaches not by rote memorization but by requiring the hearer to think and ask questions. Someone asks him a question such as "What must I do to inherit eternal life?" (Luke 10:25), and Jesus responds not with an answer but a question: "What is written in the law? What do you read there?" (Luke 10:26). Basically, Jesus says, "Put on your thinking cap. What have you learned thus far?" The lawyer then answers with the Great Commandment, and Jesus confirms its importance. But the lawyer, acting from what would seem like unspiritual motives or animus, then asks, "And who is my neighbor?" (Luke 10:29). How does Jesus answer? With a story: "Well, let me tell you about this guy who was walking on that dangerous road from Jerusalem to Jericho. You know the one." Think about it. "Oh, and by the way, the person who stops to help isn't the one you'd expect. It's a—gasp—Samaritan." And the hearers think, *What? How can that be? Samaritans aren't godly!*

That's how Jesus teaches. He tries to fully engage the mind so that we might see things in a different light. Anyone who studies the Scriptures knows we always see new and different things if we're open to the Spirit and willing to grow. If we keep asking questions, the answers keep unfolding and surprising us. The mind of Christ in a finite human being is humble. It never says, "I know what this biblical story or passage is about." Instead, the spiritual person, open to growing, always approaches the Scriptures ready to see anew what God might reveal. That attitude demonstrates that we see the Word as living. It isn't preserved like a specimen in a bottle on our shelf. It's a living, breathing Word that interacts relationally with the reader whose mind is open. The mind of Christ compels us to reflect, wonder, and study so we might see more. The mysteries of God are never fully contained within the human mind. Followers of Jesus who take on the mind of Christ never sense that we have *the* answer. We recognize there is always more to discover when it comes to reading the Bible and living according to Jesus's way. "Come and see," says Jesus (John 1:39). Keep following.

Jesus had to grow first. He studied the Scriptures and asked questions for many years. Only then did he begin to teach and challenge how people in the first century understood their lives in God and as a community. The point is clear. We're not as wise as we think we are. We've still got a lot to learn. After all, if Jesus had to grow, then as his disciples, or learners, we're called to participate in this same developmental process, even if our understanding will never be perfect. Jesus had that God's-eye view. Let the same mind be in you that was in Christ Jesus. It's worth growing into the wisdom of God. It will form you into an instrument of his love. It will heal and make whole.

Sometimes churches claim to uphold the inherited tradition of the first century or eighteenth century or whatever century is important to their beliefs. We can't change because that's what was done back then, and they had it right. As we noted earlier, it's simply not possible for us to inhabit another time and place. We can't even go back to the "way things used to be" fifty years ago, when the "church was thriving." Might it be that trying to cling to that past has led to the lack of health and vitality? Could it be that Jesus is calling us toward something new by faith, hope, and love? Have you ever gone back to your hometown after years away? Is it the same place you remember? Of course it's changed. Things are different. That's why we say "you can't go home again." And, after all, that past wasn't so glorious and perfect, if we're being honest.

If the Word is to become incarnate in our faith community here and now, twenty-first-century leaders can't view the world through first-century lenses or sixteenth-century lenses, no matter how vehemently we might claim to read the Scriptures literally. Our brains aren't designed by God to live in the past. We aren't being asked to become first-century Jews in Palestine or seventeenth-century pilgrims to the New World. We aren't asked to be followers of Paul, Martin Luther, John Wesley, or even Billy Graham. Rather, as followers of Jesus Christ, the Word should take on flesh here and now in us and through us. When we recognize our own patterns of existence, we can begin to find an expression of Jesus's way that is faithful, hopeful, and loving—a way that expresses both the incarnation in its message of the finite, particularity of unconditional love, and the cross in its message of unity and reconciliation. We can lean into the shape of love that is calling us today. We can be people who reconcile rather than divide, who see beyond my own narrow way with the mind of Christ. The calling of a faith community is to pour out love in this world, which is the only thing that can save us from ourselves.

Here's what this means for our leadership: we can't incarnate the Word in the world unless we understand our own context, our own time and place. Remember that the religious leaders in the first century had become stuck in patterns and systems of their own making that obscured the way of love. They took God's way and then shaped it to serve their own purposes of privilege, power, and exclusion. Their rules and laws harmed countless people. Of course, they couldn't see what they were doing to others and to themselves. It seemed right at the time. But they didn't have the unified perspective of the mind of Christ. So much so that they couldn't hear Jesus's message. Whatever "reformer" might be the founder of your tradition, in breaking away, they were rejecting the way rules served some and harmed others. The problem, of course, is that their "new way," like all human constructs, ultimately falls short of Jesus's way of love. They set up new rules that do harm.

Whenever people are closed off to learning, the likely outcome is rejecting Jesus all over again. Whenever we feel compelled to state our position more loudly, it's a sign that we might need to stop and listen. Trapped within their own hearts and religious systems, the religious authorities in the first century, the ones who presumed to have the answers, couldn't see Jesus was the Messiah. Instead, they clung to religious systems that they, themselves, had cobbled together on top of the way God had given to them. Human systems are always self-serving or self-referential, at least in seeking to perpetuate and sustain themselves and their way of living. Our religious containers tend to conceal God's way as much as to reveal it. That's the messy reality of being human. We often aren't any better than those first-century leaders.

What if God calls a particular system, this or that way of being religious, to die or at least to change so that something new and more faithful might emerge? I'm not suggesting we create a new denomination with a new set of rules that serve some and not others. I'm not suggesting we throw out the wisdom of the past. Instead, this is about a local, finite faith community living, moving, and being who it is called to be in time, space, and history. The faith community we lead is our focus. It's not our calling to compare ourselves to other faith communities. It's not our calling to cling to the past: "Unless a grain of wheat falls into the earth and dies, it remains just a single grain; but if it dies, it bears much fruit" (John 12:24). I like the way Eugene Peterson's *The Message* paraphrase concludes this passage in verse 25: "In the same way, anyone who holds on to life just as it is destroys that life. But if you let it go, reckless in your love, you'll have it forever, real and eternal."[14] Our religious systems are not the fullness of life in God and don't fully express Jesus's way, no matter how vehemently we uphold that system and its norms. A local faith community has the potential to love widely and wildly in the vicinity where it is born, grows, changes, and learns to love.

Human Beings Learn Collectively

If we want to grow, and help our faith community grow, by faith and hope into the future of love God places before us, then we need to be careful readers of how human beings experience the world at any given time. We need to see how human consciousness or understanding has grown and developed over the past two thousand years. We need to understand and think about who we are as twenty-first-century people. Here, we're not talking about generational differences. That's something we'll consider in chapter 4 when we discuss cultures. We are asking about human consciousness, the big picture of what we know collectively. How have human beings been formed to see the world today, which might be different from the early Christians or the Reformers in the sixteenth century? As Bryson helps us understand, "The biggest part of seeing isn't receiving visual images; it's making sense of them."[15]

By its very nature, the brain is designed to take experiences and sensory input and make meaning out of them. Our brains are always comparing sensory input to things we have already experienced. Think of the old story of the blindfolded people touching an elephant and explaining what it is. We fill in gaps, we find explanations, and we make sense of our world. But just like the blindfolded people, we can't see the big, unified picture. Maybe if we start to share what we know and how we see across time and different places, our understanding will change. The way we make sense of our world also changes over time. Don't we see things quite differently as adults than as teenagers? Our human minds change over time,[16] though because, collectively, it's a process that occurs over centuries, these shifts are not so much experienced personally but come to light as we study human history from a distance.

We are focused here on the Western perspective as it relates especially to life in the United States. How do we make meaning out of our experience in the world today? There are three major eras of intellectual development and multiple movements within each era. But for our purposes, we only need to draw out the broad, overarching patterns present in each: the premodern, the modern, and now the emerging postmodern viewpoint.[17] Let's look at how human beings, collectively, have learned new things and changed the way we understand the world and our place within it.

How Our Minds Have Changed since Jesus's Day

Our human brains have been created by God to learn, grow, develop, and change. It's not unlike being called by God to ministry. Our ministry unfolds over time in the going, doing, and living. The destination isn't given at the moment we're called. We want to be faithful and discerning in following Jesus, and that surely involves holding fast to what is true. As followers of Jesus, we hold fast to the ultimate nature and goodness of the truth of God and God's revelation in Scripture. But at times, we mistakenly hold up "my truth" or "my biblical interpretation" as precisely God's. We let animus or wrong motives shape the truth to serve our needs. Somehow, we need a bigger picture, a unified perspective, one that is less dualistic and divisive. We need the mind of Christ and the help of the Spirit. But we also need to understand the past and where we've come from on this human journey. It's really a question of knowledge—how we know what is true—and a complicated one at that. But let's see if we can get a better idea of how human beings come to some notion of what is true.

If truth were something grasped by rote memorization, if we simply needed to memorize the whole of the Scriptures, then the process would be clear. But remember that Jesus taught by telling stories and parables to make us think. We all know there are parables that almost defy understanding (the shrewd manager, anyone?). Sure, we can always come to a conclusion about what it means, but that doesn't make it the "right" answer. Our answer probably raises more questions, if we are, or our tradition is, willing to let those questions be asked. Jesus invites us into a process of learning and going deeper, as if to say, "Truth is harder and more complicated than you know. But if you'll stay open and keep digging, things will become clearer."

So many of Jesus's teachings rocked the boat, rather than setting it straight. They turned upside down what God's people thought to be true. Samaritans were "bad people," but then Jesus tells a story where a Samaritan, not their own righteous and godly people, is the only one showing compassion, generosity, and presence. Jesus touches an unclean person, and he reverses the law's logic: instead of him becoming unclean, the excluded person is made clean. He eats with a despised tax collector. He lets a woman of questionable status anoint his body (and even her questionable status might not have been so true, but how dare a woman?). These were shocking statements. And then, on top of that, Jesus says, "You've heard it said . . . but I say" (Matt. 5:21–48). If we are being faithful, Jesus is still saying that phrase to us. Get over yourself and your certainty so the Spirit can teach you new things. Start with questions, not answers. Ponder a story you've been told a hundred times. We don't have a God's-eye view of the universe, but we can grow in that wisdom and knowledge.

But if "my mind is made up," then there's not much even God can do. Our free will gives us the choice to harden our heart or to keep it pliable and open to God. What an interesting phrase: my mind is made up, as if we are making it up rather than letting go of our false constructs and missteps. We see in a mirror dimly, and if we're not careful, all we'll see is our own reflection. Remember, those ancient people tried to nail God down and to fix firmly what they believed to be true. They sought to put to death the truth that disrupted their lives and upset their way of believing and understanding God's truth. But it didn't work. God always has the last word, no matter how hard we try to preserve our own limited perspective.

The truth is that human beings see things differently over time. Many today recognize that the worldwide web is changing the brains of people, especially those who have grown up with the internet. Studies show that we have a much harder time with sustained concentration because we jump from website to website, hyperlink to hyperlink, scanning information or pictures.[18] While it might seem unsettling that reading an entire book is becoming difficult for people, we do have to ask whether our brains are developing new ways of seeing and understanding. The meaning we make of our world isn't fixed. It changes, even as we hold fast to the way revealed in Jesus Christ. That way is the standard or the anchor that allows us to move and change without losing our center.

Think about things like cell phones and laptops, the Webb telescope sweeping through deepest space, or even something as simple as a microwave. If I had to build from scratch my own microwave or cell phone, let alone an interstellar telescope, it would never happen. But human beings, collectively, now understand how to make these things. And knowledge, once discovered, never becomes unknown—though, interestingly, in the past when no documentation existed, we did lose the knowledge of how to build things such as pyramids. Knowledge and understanding are cumulative in individuals and the human species. We build layer on layer. We learn what to preserve and what to discard, though in Christ, the goal is to learn what is good and life-giving and discard what isn't. Not all knowledge is conducive to human flourishing, which is why Jesus tries to show us how to live and what to uphold.

The Premodern Mindset

Our Christian faith emerges in what is called the *premodern era*. The books of both the Old and New Testaments were written in this era. During the centuries before the Enlightenment, the spiritual dimension of life was cultivated and valued in people's lives and communities. Virtually everyone was spiritually attuned or open to the Spirit, though we shouldn't conclude that they fully grasped what the Spirit was teaching. A belief in the divine was the basis for knowing how to live together, and it's during the premodern era that universities considered theology to be the "queen of the sciences," the unifying discipline of all disciplines, we might say. All of life, including science, was governed by belief in God and God's sovereignty.

But the premodern mind and this openness to the Spirit, thanks again to our finite human nature, also upheld things like the "divine rights" of kings and queens. They believed in the Great Chain of Being that placed some people higher than others and human beings higher than any other life form. This led to many problems and abuses. It allowed those in power to tell those who were poor and disenfranchised that God had assigned them their lowly place in life. They claimed it wasn't society that marginalized them and kept them "in their place"; it was God. It's not hard to see how easily such systems can lead to harm.

But the other important piece of this premodern mindset is the limited presence of scientific methods and reasoning things through. Communal value and meaning-making were the norm. Individuals understood themselves first as a member of the whole rather than a separate individual. Thus, those who held power in society were the makers of meaning. What they told everyone was "true" was thought to be exactly as God intends. You can't argue with God. As a result, even though Galileo might have figured out that the earth actually does revolve around the sun, the religious authorities could condemn his discovery as unfaithfulness.

Premodern people inhabited what is often called a magical or mythic world shaped by the stories passed down by our ancestors within largely illiterate cultures. Those of us who preach understand the importance of telling stories to convey truth. Sometimes stories are the best way to get a sense of what's true. After all, Jesus himself taught that way, consistent with the premodern way of teaching and learning. But Jesus was teaching about the spiritual: Who is God? Who has God created us to be, and where do we fall short? How should we live if we are rightly connected to God and others? These questions of the meaning of life with and in God are the truths that Jesus offers us and hopes to reveal.

Premodern people lived in a world largely without scientific explanations, which means that physical phenomena were often explained as "spiritual" matters. Think of the Bible and the stories of demon possession. Were there actually great numbers of demons manifesting themselves in those ancient societies? Or perhaps, lacking a scientific understanding of physical and mental illness, they only knew to describe such things within the framework of a mythic world where angels and demons were actively shaping daily life. Human beings always seek to make sense of their world, and we will use whatever we "know" to provide those answers. The premodern mindset was steeped in a way of knowing that wasn't scientifically true. Yet that mythic worldview, with its suggestion that there is more than just physical matter, opened people to the spiritual, to God, to mystery, to something more than that which can be grasped fully by finite creatures.

Myths aren't something made up, like a fairy tale with a princess. They speak of something deep within the human being that rings true to who we are. A myth might not be scientifically or historically verifiable, but it can still present a true understanding of human beings in relationship to God and others. When I hear the story, I see myself and other people in it. It rings true to experience. While the premodern understanding of the universe—including biblical depictions of natural phenomena—is no longer tenable given our scientific knowledge, the myths continue to speak truly about what it means to be human and how to live in this world. Science doesn't teach us how to love. Science doesn't teach us the power of God's forgiveness. Science doesn't teach us how to be compassionate. These ancient ways of knowing were connected to mystery, to love, to the divine. The Bible does contain certain historical truths, but what is most significant about these texts is the spiritual wisdom located in our awareness and experience of the reality of God.[19]

Again, within the mythic mindset of premodernity arose all the great religious traditions with their teachings about what it means to be fully human, to live in an imperfect world, and to connect with the transforming power of the divine. Maybe God wanted human beings to first learn the way of the Spirit. We talk about putting God first in our lives. This phrase seems to speak also to human life collectively across history. For followers of Jesus, the way of love found in Jesus Christ arose amid this premodern worldview, and we are still shaped by this mythic worldview and its *spiritual* claims about how to live well and fully with God and others.

Yet this premodern perspective with its spiritual truth needs to be deepened and complemented by each successive era of human understanding. We are simply not premodern people. If we don't or won't see how human beings learn and change collectively, then it's easy to argue that the earth is only four thousand years old, the is Bible telling us the literal truth, and science is a lie. Of course, we do know that the earth is much, much older. We do know that science—while far from perfect—teaches us and shows us important things. Faith in Jesus Christ is not about disputing scientific evidence. Jesus himself rejects the premodern explanations of physical conditions that considered certain people unworthy of God, unhealthy, unnatural, unclean. He turns around and heals people over the objections of those who believed they knew and upheld the "truth." If we cling to premodern understandings of how things work, then we also will continue to accept the abuses and harm done to others in the name of God.

The Modern Mindset

Beginning in the late seventeenth and early eighteenth centuries, modern thinkers began to see the problems of those hierarchical societies that justified abuses and harm in the name of God. Human beings began to acknowledge that our minds could think and reason things through as individuals. In modernity, people turned to scientific inquiry as a corrective. And don't forget that this scientific model leads to the historical critical method of biblical interpretation, in which we recognize the context of the culture and history in which different parts of the Bible took shape. The premodern mind held to an idea of truth expressed in myths; the modern sought truth through verifiable scientific procedures. Is one way of understanding the universe a better way? Let's avoid the sin of comparisons and instead conclude that they are equally important and valuable ways of knowing—and both come with potential pitfalls.

Just like the premodern understanding of the world, the modern view is partial, incomplete, and even biased. Here's why. One of the key notions of modernity is that a universal consciousness or perspective exists and can be discovered. There is a single way of knowing the world and how we should live and act, and it can be discovered and known apart from relying on God. Moral standards can be discovered solely through human reason, the modern person says with confidence. We'll all agree if we just think about it. Each of us will come to the same conclusion.

Philosopher Louis Dupré explains that rationalism and emancipationism are the twin pillars of modern thinking. Put more simply, the modern way of life is based on: 1) the capacity to reason or think as individuals and through scientific inquiry rather than being told what to think by authorities and 2) the freedom of the individual apart from the power of the privileged, elite, rich members of society (including religious systems) to determine how we'll live our lives.[20] You can see how this pushes back against the ideas of God assigning our place in the world according to those in power. It begins to uphold the rights and the flourishing of those who are poor, marginalized, and disenfranchised, which is truly more consistent with Jesus's way. It's not hard to see that this shift in human thinking contributed to human flourishing in some important ways. Those changes put us on a path that has allowed marginalized, disempowered peoples to claim their God-given humanity in the face of oppression.

But the modern assumptions are not without their own problems and abuses. Although the intellectual history that unfolds in the modern era is complicated and ambiguous—it contains streams that reject both reason and personal autonomy—today our modern minds too often emphasize my own thinking, my own way of living, and that I owe nothing to anyone except myself. At its worst, the modern mindset upholds *my* way of thinking and living at the expense of the common good—*my personal* Lord and Savior, who becomes an individual possession in a consumeristic society.

The modern way of seeing the world can create a very self-centered individual. We can stand with arms crossed knowing the truth, unwilling to learn and grow. No doubt this attitude doesn't well represent the teachings of Jesus. It's hard to love God and others well when I'm spiraling inward into my own mind and clinging to my own heart. Drawing on Saint Augustine, both Martin Luther and Dietrich Bonhoeffer spoke of sin in terms of the Latin phrase "the heart turned in upon itself" (*cor curvum en se* or *incurvatus in se*). That pretty much captures the problem of modernity: too much *me* and not enough *us*. What's inside me is a pretty narrow view of the truth. I'm so busy protecting my heart, my truth, my way that I can't see the truth of God and neighbor. It is the source of the sin of comparisons.

Dupré illustrates the way that cultural differences have been viewed from the inside out: we begin with *my own* experience and use that to interpret and understand other ways of living. We've come to view others not through the eyes of Christ or even through someone else's eyes but only through our own personal lenses. We take what we know within ourselves and hold that up as the truth, universally. Then we judge others against the standard of myself, my ideas, my way, my practices, my life. Jesus then becomes *my personal* Lord and Savior, conformed to my life rather than calling us to conform to the way of love. Remember, that particular phrase isn't found in the Bible. It's a statement of the height of the modern impulses. The point of the scriptural witnesses is to remind us that the way, the truth, and the life is found only when we are radically related to God and others. Too much of *me* and, well, I've pretty much made an idol of myself. We like to make God in our own image rather than learning to be formed into the image of God.

It almost seems that our contemporary context and our churches sometimes set up the idol of the self in place of God. We judge and point fingers and defend our way rather than illuminating and living in love. *Only my church has it right.* You might want to ask if this is the way your church views things. *We welcome you to our church as long as you think, act, and worship just as we do.*[21] Or, instead, maybe your faith community says, "Welcome. We want to learn from and with you. What do you know about Jesus? Let's see who we might become together."

Despite the clear individualistic downside to the modern point of view, science and the rise of human rights remain life-giving contributions that need not conflict with the spiritual awareness of the premodern traditions we inherit. Faith and science are not opposed. They are different pieces of the truth of God. The premodern gives us spiritual wisdom; then the modern opens us to science that can explain some of the mysteries of God's created universe. We need all the wisdom and insight and knowledge we can get, but modernity isn't the last word in human insight and truth.

The Post-Modern Mindset

In the late twentieth and into the twenty-first centuries, post-modernity begins to enter the human conversation about what is true as it points out the fallacy of modernity's "universal" way of being human. Postmodern thinkers suggest that the modern scientific approach isn't always as fair and unbiased as some might claim. In fact, it's downright subjective at times; that is, scientific truth has often been about the experience and perspective of individuals with power and privilege. We know, for example, that medical knowledge often considered white bodies or men as "standard" and didn't study the effects of treatments or medications on people of color or women, for whom these scientific advances might work differently. Consider, too, the use of Black bodies by the powerful for the sake of scientific experimentation without regard to the harm done to them.[22]

Scientific inquiry is also partial and limited. It's why the postmodern perspective begins to address how systems and social locations function in our lives. How we view and interact with the world is inescapably tied to cultural and social norms and networks, and often we're unaware of their profound influence. Science doesn't see with a God's-eye view but with a limited human perspective and social constructs. And science can't explain every mystery. Often in modernity, not unlike premodernity, whoever held power in an institution (whether government, academia, social organizations, or, yes, the church) was able to claim that their truth was the "real" or universal truth to which others who lacked power or voice should conform. It wasn't because God gave them that role but because "science" said certain people are, by nature, better suited to power than others. Think about scientific analyses of human skulls to "prove" that the so-called Caucasian race is superior. The survival of the fittest clearly shows that men are to rule over women as the "weaker sex." Science isn't always as pure as we'd like it to be. Here we can see a possible explanation for the growing distrust of institutions of all kinds, especially among younger generations. Marginalized peoples have always known that this power dimension holds sway and that it's not the only way to see the world and live within it.[23]

The full shape of what we'll learn in this emerging postmodern era is yet to be revealed. But there are some pieces of the puzzle that can be put forth. The postmodern mind suggests that no human being or group of human beings can claim to have the full understanding of what it means to be human and how we "ought" to live. In the modern period, whoever held power and had a voice got to decide what's universal and "the right or best" approach to human existence. But we know that power over others isn't the way of love, which empties itself and becomes the servant of all. Thus, the emerging postmodern era helps to illuminate further what Jesus was teaching.

The post-modern perspective shows us that we live in various cultural contexts—though often unaware of them—and they shape and mold our experiences, as well as what and how we know. We might suggest that the premodern put us in touch with mystery and spirituality as the first layer of collective wisdom, the modern opened us to scientific explanations of natural phenomena as the second layer, and the postmodern helps us realize we are always socially and communally formed, interwoven, and interconnected beings such that what is true is found in relationship to others and the whole of creation.

So here we are, modern people in the process of being reshaped and reformed according to an emerging postmodern perspective. Think about what this might mean alongside the idea that we followers of Jesus are in the midst of an every-five-hundred-year reformation. Then add into the mix the heightened sense of being globally connected and concerned. Plus, the rate of technological change in the past fifty or one hundred years has been exponential, astronomical.[24] It's a time of change, especially in terms of how we understand ourselves, our world, our God, and what is true. No wonder there is so much societal turmoil, conflict, and division. A new layer of human understanding is emerging.

Even so, we're often unaware of the formative pull of modern assumptions, considering them as simply "the way things are" when, in fact, they're not the only way to understand the world in which we live. That's why things might seem unsettled and uncomfortable. Becoming aware of this context is central to the faith journey and to leading faith communities in the way of love. The human mind will always see and know the world in part. But it can and does learn and grow. That's the process God created. We're aiming to grow into the mind of Christ, a more unified, wholistic, and life-giving perspective than Jesus's followers could possess in the past. We need each layer of wisdom to be more closely aligned with the way God sees all things. Each layer is a gift from God, as if revealing to us something else that helps us more fully understand the world God has created and our calling in Jesus Christ to overflow with love.

In the context of a faith community, the way we do something isn't the only way it can be done faithfully, and yet we often assume that what makes me comfortable is the "right" way. Certainly, countless generations of Christians have imposed cultural norms on other peoples—things like clothing or hairstyles—which have nothing to do with Jesus's teachings and nothing to do with love. Often, we've done more harm than good in offering Christ because we were unable to see the water we were swimming in. We assume our way of life is the way of Jesus. But there are many ways to be a faith community and follow Jesus Christ. It begins with learning to see more fully, to ask questions, and to avoid the sin of comparisons. We let the Word become flesh here and now.

When we fail to grasp that we are shaped by particular cultural and social systems, we open ourselves to doing harm to others. We exchange the way of love for social constructions that include some and exclude others, often based on physical characteristics or the way they've been created by God. We often become divisive and defensive, which tears down the way of love. We view others as a threat to our way rather than as one expression of God's way incarnate in the world.

This sketch of Western intellectual history is an oversimplification, of course. It doesn't begin to address how people around the globe have understood and do understand life on earth. The main point to keep in mind is that successive generations of human beings can and do understand and approach the world with new and different lenses than our ancestors could and did. We take the truth of the past that endures and enables life to flourish, and we add new insights. It's as Isaiah suggests: God goes before us and announces, "I am about to do a new thing; now it springs forth, do you not perceive it?" (Isa. 43:19). We are not static, unchanging creatures possessing the full knowledge or wisdom of God and the universe. Ours is a journey of discovery or learning to see anew. Leading with love is about living into the future promised by God and being open to learn and grow.

Growing in Faith Grows Us in Love

Somehow, we've gotten the notion that numbers are the measure of spiritual health in the church. The bigger the better. That notion of "more is better" isn't God's measure of faithfulness. Some faith communities that are filled with the Spirit are overflowing with people. But a small, rural faith community can also be filled with the Spirit and learning to love God and others well. Numbers are not a good measure of faithfulness or spiritual growth. God asks us, as leaders of faith communities, to grow our people spiritually. So stop asking other pastors how many members they have or how large their congregation is. It doesn't matter to God. That's the sin of comparisons. More than, less than, better than, worse than. We aren't in a competition when it comes to leading God's people. If you have ten people in your faith community, lead them well. If you have ten thousand people, lead them well. Maybe we should be asking: How well is your faith community serving beyond the walls? What are they learning about Jesus's way? Are they participating in the reconciliation of all things? Are they growing in their love of God and others? After all, the Great Commandment should be the measure that matters for our leadership.

Brian McLaren's book *Faith after Doubt* provides a framework to identify and move our faith community forward. As spiritual leaders and guides, our own growth and development should be taken seriously rather than as a box we check on an annual report about our continuing education. How can you expect to lead people deeper into God if you, yourself, aren't going deeper? How seriously do you take your own relationship with God? The spiritual dimension of human life is the priority as all else flows from that relationship. Personal spiritual growth, paradoxically, isn't about making me holy so much as it's a recognition that I can't love God and others unless I'm spending adequate time with God so that I might be reformed and remade to better lead God's people along the way of love.

Let me try to simplify McLaren's framework as he wrestles with multiple theories of faith development. He's not inventing the idea that people can and do grow in faith but helping to illuminate and clarify how our spiritual development happens. Our faith community will consist of people in different stages of faith, but a community will tend toward one collective stage or another. One of the most important insights McLaren offers is the idea that doubt is the fuel that fires our spiritual growth. Sometimes doubt gets a bad rap as being the opposite of faith. But McLaren helps us to see that doubt is a component of faith because when we wrestle with our questions, we come to a deeper sense of God's mystery and immensity that allows us to rest more deeply in that faith. Good leaders know how to introduce enough doubt to help people wrestle with their faith but not so much as to cause them to become closed to growing.

McLaren recognizes that theorists such as James Fowler and Carol Gilligan provide different developmental frameworks for our growth in faith. He brings together these insights and describes four stages of faith he calls *simplicity, complexity, perplexity,* and *harmony.* These stages help us discern our own stage of development as well as our faith community's stage, which, in turn, gives us insights into where we might need to grow and what sort of doubt will aid that process.

In stage-one faith, or simplicity, "you set out to master the mental skills of dualism, of seeing the world in twos: this or that, in or out, right or wrong."[25] Here we find the kind of us-versus-them mentality that is often the source of conflict and division. In this earliest stage, we depend on the expertise of authorities and repeat what we've been taught to think and speak. It's all so simple: just trust and obey, for there's no other way. But whom are we obeying? That's the real question. McLaren notes that simplicity works well for children—in some sense, stage one is necessary to create a moral framework—but in adolescence (or much later), as our brains mature, we might begin to ask some questions about what we've been taught. A dash of doubt and we begin to see things we haven't before.

In stage two, or what McLaren calls *complexity,* we ask pragmatic questions such as "What good is being good if I don't get the rewards of being good?"[26] We all know people who are disappointed that they've done and believed everything they are "supposed" to do and believe, but their lives still aren't achieving success and aren't "better" than nonbelievers' lives. Stage two, then, is about being effective or successful. It's about winning in life. No longer focused on right/wrong as our framework, it's now success/failure that drives us. It makes me think about the twentysomething seminary student who is convinced they should be pastor of the largest church in the territory because their enthusiasm, activism, and confidence will win the day. Of course, they soon discover, in a much smaller setting, that perhaps they were somewhat naïve. What happens when we begin to question this results-oriented framework for our faith? What happens when growing the church numerically, as our measure of success, brings more problems, conflicts, and stress than it brings joy and peace and love? When we realize we've managed to achieve more church and less life in God? More people but not necessarily more of the Spirit?

At this point, our doubt and questions become the doorway to stage three, or *perplexity*, according to McLaren. In stage three, people now find life more mysterious, and truth is not as simple and clear-cut as we once assumed. Stage three can be considered a place where we begin to view things as more relative, less certain and fixed, and often in need of critique. McLaren admits that congregations who mature to this stage "tend to self-destruct in five different ways."[27] Stage-three people distrust institutions and want to deconstruct them; they distrust authority figures, including their pastor; they analyze things more than they set goals and undertake missions; they're not sure the group norms are something to which they can belong; and they operate out of suspicion and scrutiny.[28] So much doubt, so many questions.

Sometimes stage-three people end up regressing because the instability of such questioning and skepticism is too much. McLaren even refers to stage three as "descent," given that a faith crisis often triggers this stage.[29] But if negotiated well, a person will mature into stage-four faith, *harmony.* Harmony is a place of "nondiscriminatory love."[30] In harmony, the dualisms that we have lived with, those ways of thinking that divide and categorize, now become fluid. We aren't driven by the sin of comparisons. We recognize that there is more to see on both sides than we've been taught, and in fact, there are more than two ways of viewing life and faith. In harmony, "we find not meaninglessness and banality but profound, inexpressible belovedness and beauty."[31] Richard Rohr's teaching that "everything belongs" is an apt phrase.[32] We see that God created everything, the universe is woven together, and we are all one, or radically related. McLaren concludes that "doubt prepares the way for a new kind of faith after (and with) doubt, a humbled and harmonious faith, a faith that expresses itself in love."[33] Growing into the fullness of love is a long and often difficult process, but it's the way of Jesus, if we will open ourselves to go on this journey. Until we grow beyond a dualistic mindset, we'll never express the fullness of love.

When we acknowledge that both individuals and faith communities are developmental by nature, that we are created to grow and change, the purpose of leadership emerges. We don't lead for the sake of increasing the numbers in the sanctuary (though that can be a tangible outcome). We don't lead to keep the people happy, to be liked, or to climb a denominational or other ladder of our making. We don't lead to preserve the way we've always done things. We don't lead to prove we are right or in charge or holier or whatever outcome you might have in mind. We lead to enable others to grow in the way of love: to be healed, whole, and deeply interconnected with all that is. Such development begins with the leader pursuing a deeper understanding and practice of the way of love since you can't lead people to a place you haven't journeyed yourself. What stage are you in, Pastor? And are you willing to take the next step along the way? It may not be easy, but the summit beckons you. As for the faith community you lead, the one thing necessary for you to help them grow is love. If they trust that you love them unconditionally, they'll be able to absorb some discomfort as you help them to question, to doubt, and to grow. We are designed by God to learn, grow, and change.

Practice Makes (More but Not Completely) Perfect

1. Can you identify which stage, according to McLaren, you might be in? What about your faith community? How would you describe the overall stage of the group?
2. How are you growing in your own understanding of Scripture, God, your people? How do you open yourself to mystery? Do you have a plan for growing?
3. How is your faith community growing in its understanding and practice of the faith? Do your sermons challenge the people to think more carefully and deeply about their lives in God and with others? Or do you simply reiterate what you think they want to hear? Can you see small steps forward for them to consider new questions? Can you develop a plan for gradually growing their doubt and faith?

4. Can you think of a time or situation when you pushed your faith community too far? A time when leading with love meant you should have taken a smaller step? What did that help you to see or learn?

Resources for Going Deeper

Beck, Don Edward, and Christopher C. Cowan. *Spiral Dynamics: Mastering Values, Leadership, and Change.* New York: John Wiley and Sons, 2014.

McLaren, Brian. *Faith after Doubt: Why Your Beliefs Stopped Working and What to Do about It.* New York: St. Martin's, 2021.

Wilber, Ken. *Integral Spirituality: A Startling New Role for Religion in the Modern and Postmodern World.* Boulder, CO: Integral Books, 2006.

❧ 2 ❧

DEEP LISTENING

Leadership Principle Three: Stay open to the Spirit and listen deeply

I LOVE TO hike on mountain trails. There is something soul-satisfying about the beauty and immensity of those peaks, the crunch of hiking boots on the path, the scent of pine trees, and even the altitude dragging on my body that connects me to God and the cosmos. Sometimes when I start off, I'm distracted and deep within my thoughts. But gradually, I become attuned to the natural world and sink into it, as if remembering I'm created from the same stuff as these mountains. I become still within my soul, and there is more room for the Spirit. My atoms and molecules become enlivened or vivified. I remember how to listen. I become my breath and my beating heart. In that still place, startling things can happen.

Once as I was quietly descending alone along a trail, I rounded a bend and came face to face with a magnificent doe three feet in front of me on the trail. We both froze, and as I stood motionless, she walked around the large bush to the side of the trail and then got back on the trail behind me. If I had been noisy and unfocused, I would have missed this stunning moment of connection. Even more, there is no way to capture and preserve the experience in its fullness. It simply dwells within my mind, heart, and spirit, and no photos can replicate the full experience. But each experience in life—the interweaving of thoughts, feelings, sight, sound, taste, smell—leaves a mark on my soul, where it lives on throughout my days on earth. I can replay that tape whenever I choose.

The Scriptures are clear in their advice: Be still and know that I am God (Ps. 46:10). Silence is a gateway to encountering God. Unfortunately, we tend to live in a way that puts up a barrier between us and that still, small voice. Our cell phones, TVs, streaming music, podcasts, and so on are a constant presence that keeps us at arm's length from listening to God. We are too often surrounded by the constant hum of refrigerators and HVAC systems, cars and trucks in motion, weed whackers and lawn mowers. So many sounds of human making that keep silence at bay. We can't hear for all the noise. Silence requires intentionality.

If you're a pastor, you know the importance of listening. Listening is part of what we call the *ministry of presence*. We have to be fully present to others. In fact, it might be the single most important pastoral skill when it comes to building relationships of trust. Imagine you're meeting with a member of your faith community who is in the midst of grief or crisis. But while you're together, you spend the whole time checking, even briefly, each text that arrives on your cell phone. You might think you're listening, but you'd be distracted and not fully present. That grieving person would certainly know you aren't present. Or maybe you've observed a parent out walking with their children but talking on their cell phone. Maybe they even snap a photo of the walk and post it on social media. The child knows that parent has been with them but not present to them.

Somehow, we convince ourselves, it's different with God. I can be doing and scrolling, attending to every interruption, working on my sermon in the midst of life's cacophony, confident I'm hearing God's still, small voice. But the truth is our relationship with God has to be cultivated attentively, in quiet listening, just as any other relationship requires our full presence. Often in life, our most profound moments with a loved one are simply sitting side by side in silence. Simply present with one another. That's awkward if your relationship is superficial. And maybe that's a good indicator of how comfortable our spirit is with God. Can we be still and know? Growing in love means making the effort to give our undivided attention to God on a regular basis. To be present. Our third leadership principle is to stay open to the Spirit and listen deeply.

Maybe for you, the doorway to silence is found when lounging beside a serene lake with a fishing rod or strolling along the beach with waves crashing on the shore and an occasional gull crying out. If you're an urban dweller, it might be birdwatching in Central Park or just sitting in the cool of the evening and watching the sunset. We often talk about pastors going on retreat, taking a sabbath, and unwinding in nature. The beauty of creation has a way of restoring the soul and reconnecting us with God and, sometimes, ourselves. It reminds us of who we are and whose we are. When we take a break from our busy lives, from the demands of leadership, and from our ubiquitous forms of technology, our spiritual senses are reawakened from their slumber. This chapter furthers our journey of leading with love by reminding us that we must honor our own spiritual journey so that we might be sustained in our ministry. Yes, it's cliché, but we really should put on our own oxygen mask first. Those daily moments of quiet listening, present to God without any agenda, are the stuff of growth in the Spirit. When we are deeply connected to the Spirit, we can accompany others into those depths. When we are deeply connected to the Spirit, love is present.

If you've been in ministry for any length of time, you've experienced the birth or baptism of a tiny infant, as well as the privilege of sitting beside someone making the transition from this life to the next. The baby's first breath marks the entryway into the gift of human life. The dying person's last breath signifies the end of a sojourn on earth. But in between, under normal circumstances, we mostly forget about our breathing. It's our breath that vivifies us. Our breath makes us alive. It is truly a connection point with life itself. In Genesis, God breathes on the earth creature (*ha-adam*), and it becomes a living being (Gen. 2:7). In the valley of dry bones, Ezekiel prophesies, and the bones rattle back together. Then "the breath came into them, and they lived" (Ezek. 37:10). In Jesus's resurrection appearances, he breathes on the disciples as if to reanimate their souls and restore the breath of life: "Jesus said to them again, 'Peace be with you. As the Father has sent me, so I send you.' When he had said this, he breathed on them" (John 20:21–22). And when he says, "Peace be with you," he's saying, "*Shalom* to you." *Shalom* means nothing less than healing and wholeness. *Shalom* is Jesus offering salvation.

What a wonderful relationship exists between our breath and the Spirit. In Hebrew, the word *ruach* can be translated as "breath" or "Spirit." In Greek, the word *pneuma* can be translated as "breath" or "Spirit." The breath of life is a connection point to the Spirit. We can't hold on to or keep or possess our breath. We have to let it go. Breathing is central to receiving the Spirit. Our breath is the trailhead to the way of love. Remembering our breath, taking the time to pay attention to our breathing, is a spiritual practice. It's a contemplative pause that opens us to the still, small voice so that we might discover God and ourselves more deeply.

Do you remember the story of Elijah fleeing from Jezebel after serving God's purposes in defeating the eight hundred priests of Baal (1 Kgs. 19)?[1] In his exhaustion, spiritually depleted, Elijah hears a secondhand threat that Jezebel will take his life, and he rushes headlong into the desert, where he lies down under a broom tree, ready to die. Pretty easy to forget how God has been working with and through us when some new challenge or threat appears, isn't it? Plus, you have to wonder if Elijah took any time off to restore himself in the midst of doing all this work for God. Despite his burn-out, angels sustain him, though the text is unclear as to whether he sees the angel or just the sustenance, and then Elijah continues running away from his ministry and himself right up to a cave high on the mountain.

Of course, Elijah runs right into God and his own fears, exhaustion, and anxieties. In a sense, he's running from his calling. Yet he runs right into God. And the place where he encounters God is in the silence, in the still, small voice. Not in the thunder and lightning, not in the earthquake. In the sheer silence: "Be still, and know that I am God" (Ps. 46:10). Then God asks, "What are you doing here, Elijah?" (1 Kgs. 19:13). Breathe, Elijah, just breathe. Are you tired and running on empty, Pastor? Pay attention to Elijah's story. Being called doesn't mean we don't need God anymore. Being called doesn't mean we won't get tired or anxious sometimes. We need to remember to breathe. Maybe you need to encounter God in the deep silence that comes with a contemplative pause.

The Spiritual Life and Opening Our Hearts

Spirituality is essential to the way of Jesus and to loving deeply. In Luke 6:12, for example, we find Jesus stepping aside for a contemplative pause before he assembles his leadership team (the disciples): "Now during those days he went out to the mountain to pray; and he spent the night in prayer to God." We won't be able to lead with love unless we learn to "spend the night in prayer." Alone. In silence. Spirituality involves opening ourselves to the depths of Mystery. We prioritize time apart to encounter and enter into the triune, relational life that envelops us in love, that breathes life into our lungs and Spirit.

Spirituality, though, isn't easily described or explained. It's a concept that is more "caught" than "taught." But let's try to define it. Barbara Brown Taylor uses the phrase "spiritual but not religious" to tease out the meaning of *spirituality*. She acknowledges that many people "have a sense of the divine depths of things but they are not churchgoers. They want to grow closer to God, but not at the cost of creeds, confessions, religious wars large or small."[2] In attempting to use finite words to express the infinite, Taylor suggests that spirituality "may be the name for longing—for more meaning, more feeling, more connection, more life."[3] Spirituality yearns for something more.

Ronald Rolheiser likewise points to this sense of longing, or "holy longing" as he calls it. Rolheiser claims that everyone has a spirituality, "either a life-giving one or a destructive one. . . . We wake up [in this world] crying, on fire with desire, with madness. What we do with that madness is our spirituality."[4] After explaining, much like Taylor, that spirituality isn't about "anything explicitly religious," he concludes, "it's what we do with that fire, how we channel it."[5] The way we respond to that deep fire or desire or longing, "the disciplines and habits we choose to live by, will either lead to greater integration or disintegration within our bodies, minds, and souls, and to a greater integration or disintegration in the way we are related to God, others, and the cosmic world."[6] For Rolheiser, our soul is the connection point within and beyond ourselves. It's the source of integration, vitality, energy, and life.

Marjorie Thompson echoes this notion of spirituality as the source of a life that is integrated and energized: "Scripturally speaking, the spiritual life is simply the increasing vitality and sway of God's Spirit in us. It is a magnificent choreography of the Holy Spirit in the human spirit, moving us toward communion with both Creator and creation. The spiritual life is thus grounded in relationship. It has to do with God's way of relating to us and our way of responding to God."[7] Simply put, spirituality is our deep connection to God. It's our restless heart yearning for the divine to breathe within us. Faith-filled spirituality is nothing less than God's love living in us and through us. We become open to radical relationship with God, others, and all of creation. We receive life in abundance. We breathe as one. We come to see that our breath already connects us. We are created to be held together by a web of relationships in which we give and receive life. Religion or the faith community, at its best, serves this purpose. At its worst, religion and the church promulgate the ways of the world: division, conflict, dehumanization, and the diminishment of life. Our selfishness is suffocating.

There is no way to access this depth dimension without practices that enable us to listen to and for God. There is no podcast, prayer, or practice that provides spirituality in and of itself. Instead, any practice or prompt should open us to pause and simply listen. We have to stop what we're doing, thinking, and feeling. We understand that we seek God, we seek the Spirit, through intentional practices. We also understand that without our intentionality and our sheer presence, God will allow us to run away in other directions and to channel our desire and life in ways that are destructive and do harm. Yet as Scripture attests, God never stops trying to draw our hearts into the love of God that heals and makes whole and that flows from us into the suffering world to do the same.

So we worship within a community that seeks to know God and to go where the Spirit leads rather than hoping God will somehow contain the Spirit and make us comfortable. We read and study Scripture so that we might hear from God, so God's Word might take up residence within us. We don't read simply to confirm what we already "know" is "true." We fast to open ourselves to God, recognizing we live in a culture of overabundance and overconsumption. We need to trim away the excess and make room. We engage in works of mercy, going out to be the body of Christ for those who suffer and are in need. In so doing, we find ourselves emptied and filled. We practice generosity because it's like a boomerang that returns joy and happiness to our hearts. We go on retreat to reconnect to the silence and beauty of the natural world. And of course, we engage in intercessory prayer, asking that God might heal and uplift those who suffer in various ways. As Saint Augustine suggested in his *Confessions*, our hearts are restless until they rest in God.

But in our society today, filled with nonstop noise and to-do lists a mile long, we often find it difficult to settle down and be present to God. Sometimes pastors find that the easiest thing to scratch off a long list is their personal devotional life. "I'm too busy to seek God. God will understand. After all, I'm a pastor," we justify. "All of my life is dedicated to God." Yet God continues to call and ask us to stop by and sit for a spell. That time with God isn't about making me holy so others can see who I am. It's not about making me powerful or important. It's certainly not about "blessing" me with material goods. Being with God is about becoming who we are created to be. It's about stripping away our ego with all its claims and false demands, all its wounds and wounding. It's about breathing. It's about properly channeling the fire within. The depths of spirituality will change us into the image of love.

There is a practice of seeking the Spirit that presents itself as more needed today than ever. I'm not suggesting we should abandon the disciplines mentioned above. We need worship, Scripture, intercessory prayer, fasting, and so forth. We need to live a disciplined life of seeking the Spirit. The spiritual disciplines are timeless treasures that form us spiritually. But given the busyness, noisiness, and sense of "urgency" that exist in our world today, the one practice we need the most is deep listening. We need to quiet our minds. We need to quiet our texts, phones, televisions, podcasts, tunes, websites, earbuds, and everything that demands that we listen up. We need to recover and cultivate the deep listening found in contemplative prayer.

Today, we need to recover the practice of breathing. Simply breathing with the living God. *Sola Spiritus*. Spirit alone and alone with the Spirit. As the Reformation gave us *sola fides* (faith alone) and *sola scriptura* (Scripture alone), this time of reformation calls for *sola Spiritus*. It doesn't replace the wisdom of the past and the practices of the faith. It doesn't suggest being apart from the community of faith and never joining in the body of Christ. It doesn't mean to abandon Scripture or faith. But *sola Spiritus* points us back to the still, small voice. It reminds us to stop running, to be still, to listen.

Deep Listening and *Sola Spiritus*

There is a long history in the Christian tradition of contemplative prayer. Desert fathers and mothers praying in solitude in the wilderness. Mystics such as Julian of Norwich, Teresa of Avila, and Saint John of the Cross all offer glimpses of how to listen for God in silence and to quiet our constant need to think and feel this way and that. Sometimes we need just to be, even when convinced we should be doing. Contemplatives remind us never to let the to-do list become an idol before which we prostrate ourselves.

It seems clear that in the noisiness of the twenty-first century, practices of quiet contemplation are more crucial than ever. The Spirit calls to us. Unlike with premodern people, silence doesn't just happen as a normal part of life. And that should make us really ponder, given that premodern people, whose world would have been quieter, still sought silence.

But let's be clear about what contemplation is not. It's not an escape from the world or fleeing from problems. It's not about closing our ears and hearts to the world's injustice. Contemplation isn't some magic formula to fix all our worldly problems or to eliminate our personal difficulties. Contemplation isn't a practice where we expect something to happen while we are sitting in quiet. Instead, it's a practice that allows God to show us who we are and who we are meant to be. It's about seeing myself, the world, and especially God more clearly. It's about letting go of my "understanding" and expectations of God, myself, and the spiritual life, which enables me to understand and serve God and others less selfishly and more fully. It's about being drawn into the intimacy of the Trinity, the God who is relational. It draws me one breath closer to being who God created me to be for this sojourn on earth. It points away from the dualisms that create exclusions and conflict and toward the radically related oneness that is our calling and destiny. And it spins me out into the world to bring the breath of life, connection, healing, and wholeness to everything and everyone that God has created: "What a breath of fresh air you are!" Our calling is to become the very breath of life in the world. In our society, in our neighborhood, in our faith community, in our home, and in our heart, we breathe life and love.

In contemplation, we seek nothing. We simply remain open to whatever is given by God. As Richard Rohr explains, "Prayer is not primarily saying words or thinking thoughts. It is, rather, a stance. It's a way of living in the Presence, living in awareness of the Presence, and even enjoying the Presence. The contemplative is not just aware of God's Loving Presence, but trusts, allows, and delights in it."[8] Contemplation is the deepest form of listening to God as we seek to get over ourselves and see the world through the eyes of God or the "mind of Christ." We become a vessel or conduit of the Spirit as we journey through the world. We become present to everything.

The basic human problem we all face is what Dietrich Bonhoeffer, and Martin Luther before him, described as the "heart turned in upon itself."

Think about this imagery. If the heart is turned inward, protecting and focusing on itself, how can it love God and others? Someone in this condition might think they are loving and compassionate when their motives are really self-reward, self-gain, self-protection, and so forth. Often, we don't see ourselves the way others see us. In most cases, we aren't even aware of our self-focus. Our wounds, our scars, our fears, our needs form a heavy cover that weighs down our truest self so it doesn't connect with God or others. We're holding our breath, suffocating, and don't even see it. We are nowhere near as nimble as we think ourselves to be. We're dragging along a lot of baggage. But when we begin to practice contemplation, the cover that obscures our truest self gradually lifts, and our heart can turn outward to God and others, to the whole of creation, in right relationship. *Sola Spiritus.*

Isn't the traditional language of "right relationship" interesting? It doesn't indicate that "I" no longer exist. It says my relationship with God, others, and creation is "right" and good and just in the way that God intends. To lead well, to lead with love, we've got to let go of our selfishness—in whatever form it might manifest itself, including the need to be "successful" in leadership or admired by others or viewed as holy or righteous or whatever—see ourselves as we truly are, and rest in God's love whether we are being appreciated or critiqued, moving our congregation forward or feeling stuck, happy with our ministry or frustrated. We let the Spirit, the breath of life, sustain us.

Do you remember what God asks Elijah after he's run to the mountain, exhausted and fearful? Simply this: "What are you doing here, Elijah?" (1 Kgs. 19:13). It's the same question, really, that God asks the people in the garden of Eden: "Where are you?" (Gen. 3:9). God knows. It's Adam and Eve, Elijah, you, and I who aren't paying attention to where we are and why. We are called to examine and understand how our own experiences in life shape the way we see ourselves, the world, and the living God. Where we find ourselves isn't always God's doing; often it's our inability to see and hear how we are running in the wrong direction or running ourselves into the ground. Elijah is hiding in a cave because he is running from his ministry. He's running because he's afraid of the threats to his life and well-being. He's running because he's burned out. He's running from his own stuff, but he wants to blame God, telling God how faithful he's been. If we start blaming others or God, we might need to look at our own messiness first because there's a good chance we're part of the problem. When God asks, "What are you doing here?" the answer ought to be, "Listening."

So how does contemplative practice help us get to right relationship? How does this prayer of the heart enable us to strip away unhealthy layers that have accumulated over time and through our formation in various communities? Contemplation isn't a substitute for counseling and therapy. Most of us need to work through the wounds that life brings. But over time, contemplation *will* reveal those things that you might need to take up with a counselor. It makes us aware of whatever is deep within us. Thomas Keating refers to this bubbling up of emotional baggage as "the unloading of the unconscious."[9] He points to Saint John of the Cross, who "taught that interior silence is the place where the Spirit secretly anoints the soul and heals our deepest wounds."[10] What emerges is a more integrated, whole person. Contemplation doesn't just open us to God; it also opens us to ourselves in ways that allow us to heal by the grace of God.

There are many resources that can help us understand this spiritual practice of contemplation. Some of them have been part of the Christian tradition for centuries, such as Teresa of Avila's *Interior Castle*, John of the Cross's *Dark Night of the Soul*, Julian of Norwich's *Showings*, and the *Cloud of Unknowing*. There are modern classics such as *Open Mind, Open Heart* by Thomas Keating and Howard Thurman's mystical writings such as *The Luminous Darkness*. More recently still, Richard Rohr's *Just This* and *Everything Belongs* and Cynthia Bourgeault's *The Wisdom Jesus* can point us in the right direction. Those who engage regularly in contemplative practice experience it as a portal to a deeper relationship with God, others, and our truest self. And this deeper, truer relationship requires that we let go of our formative patterns and experiences that have built a wall or fence between us and God or between us and others. Never think the call to ministry or to be a follower of Jesus is about having "arrived." It's quite the opposite. The calling is to go even deeper, to seek even more intentionally the way of love. Contemplation is about settling into the still, small voice. It's what I will call *deep listening*.

So what is contemplation? How do we do this kind of deep listening? Contemplation, at its core, is placing ourselves before the mystery of

God and quieting our minds and hearts. In theological language, this is the *apophatic* way, the way of not knowing, not feeling, not expecting, not doing. Sheer abandonment into the arms of God. *Sola Spiritus.* Like an infant who is totally open and unformed in patterns of living, who has no words, no to-do list. It is, as St. John of the Cross would say, *nada*, nothing. Unconditional and full surrender to God. All our preconceived notions, all the emotions we have stored in our brain, all our expectations of who we should be and how life ought to unfold become shrouded. Ronald Rolheiser puts it this way: "Centering oneself in prayer, one simply sits, but sits inside the intention of reaching out and directly towards God in a place beyond feeling and imagination where one waits to let the unimaginable reality of God break through in a way that subjective feelings, thoughts, and imaginations cannot manipulate."[11] Contemplation is the only true path to discover ourselves naked before God, who waits to heal us and make us whole. We let go of all that we think we are and should be or do. God meets us in that stillness, in that shroud of mystery.

That deepest listening might not even enter our awareness. It is subtle, as if trying to hear fungi push up through the fertile soil in the forest. As if listening for the sound of our lungs filling with air. The movement of God within us can't be controlled or even, at times, sensed. But the Presence is working within, healing our wounds and ego-driven compulsions so that we might be fully alive and more open to live as a conduit of God's love in the suffering world.

Every person called to ministry in faith communities should read and study Henri Nouwen's *The Way of the Heart*. Nouwen teaches that "we must be made aware of the call to let our false, compulsive self be transformed . . . . solitude is the furnace in which this transformation takes place. . . . it is from this transformed or converted self that real ministry flows."[12] The first requirement of contemplation, then, is solitude. If you have a crowd of contemplatives, solitude is still possible as it's an attitude of inwardness without the need to be seen, heard, or engaged by others. Solitude is being open to hear God speak in the depths of the heart. To be still.

To solitude, we add the second ingredient: silence. True solitude does not come with earbuds, must-see streaming, the latest praise music, or any other artificial noise. Sometimes we might use music or chant to take us into a contemplative posture, but it's only a gateway to deep listening in silence. As Nouwen suggests, silence is "an indispensable discipline in the spiritual life" that counters or counteracts the wordiness of our lives in the world.[13] What I love about Nouwen's description of the practice of silence is how he articulates its fundamental importance to leading with love. "As ministers," writes Nouwen, "our greatest temptation is toward too many words."[14] Too many words and we can't hear the Word. Only when we take silence seriously do our words carry the depth of divine life: "Words can only create communion and thus new life when they embody the silence from which they emerge. As soon as we begin to take hold of each other by our words, and use words to defend ourselves or offend others, the word no longer speaks of silence. But when the word calls forth the healing and restoring stillness of its own silence, few words are needed."[15] And so Nouwen concludes that silence "is the mystery of the future world" as it "allows us to speak a word that participates in the creative and recreative power of God's own Word."[16] Silence forms us for midwifery. It forms us to lead toward God's future.

Our thoughts, feelings, and expectations too often get in the way of hearing and seeing God in our midst. The only way the depths will transform our layers of formation in the world is through silence and deep listening. Keating tells us that the experience of meeting the Divine Mystery through contemplation "is beyond the power of any [human] faculty to perceive . . . One can only remark its presence by its fruits in one's life."[17] Our work is to submit ourselves to the silence. And it's nowhere as easy as we imagine it to be. But it's also nowhere as difficult as we imagine.

Keating calls contemplative prayer "the way of pure faith" and insists that we "do not have to feel it, but [we] have to practice it."[18] It's about the intention itself. It's about surrendering ourselves utterly to God. Contemplation, in the words of Nouwen, "penetrates the marrow of our soul and leaves nothing untouched. The prayer of the heart is a prayer that does not allow us to limit our relationship with God to interesting words or pious emotions. By its very nature such prayer transforms our whole being into Christ precisely because it opens the eyes of our soul to the truth *of ourselves* as well as the truth of God."[19] Nouwen goes so far as to call this the "prayer of truth."[20] What a fascinating phrase given our current state of society, where so many feel compelled to defend their own ideas of the truth of God. Nouwen says if you're using a lot of words, you haven't yet gotten to the truth. It reminds me of the saying that's usually credited to St. Francis: Preach always; use words only when necessary. In a wordy society, only silence can begin to reveal what is true, beautiful, and worthy of our praise. And that silence causes us to hold our tongue.

In Keating's view, contemplative prayer, what I'm calling *deep listening*, is the truest form of self-denial: "Denial of our *inmost* self includes detachment from the habitual functioning of our intellect and will . . . This may require letting go not only of ordinary thoughts during prayer, but also of our most devout reflections and aspirations."[21] When we practice deep listening, God reveals our unconscious so that we can see ourselves more accurately. We are consoled in our wounds, assured in our gifts, and humbled in our weaknesses.[22] Ultimately, deep listening allows us to let go of even these consolations and humiliations and to dwell in detachment or emptiness. Utterly surrendered to God. *Sola Spiritus*. Yes, there's a paradox here. Our deepest and truest connection to God comes when we let go of "God," or the God we have made in our own image. Again, Keating warns or encourages us that it's not about what we feel or think but only a matter of consistent, intentional practice. I can't tell you how many times I've heard students say, "Nothing is happening." And I respond, "Yes."

Practices of Deep Listening

If you read books on contemplation, you'll discover there are different ways to engage in deep listening. *Lectio Divina*, deep listening to Scripture, is a contemplative practice as long as it leads to a period of sustained silence and sheer openness. Thelma Hall's *Too Deep for Words* is a modern classic on the practice.[23] Sitting quietly in nature can be a means of deep listening. But here we will introduce one of the most common contemplative practices: centering prayer and some variations on the theme. The most important consideration is to find what works for you to cultivate that place of silent attentiveness and openness. To engage in centering prayer, we want to find a comfortable chair and put our feet on the ground while our backs are straight and our hands relaxed. Close the eyes or fix them gently on the ground. Take several slow, deep breaths, filling the belly like a balloon, holding the breath, and then slowly releasing it.

Now comes the hard part, which is getting our monkey mind—the thoughts and feelings that incessantly chatter away—to move on. They often won't stop, but we don't let them hold our attention. The technique for gently pushing all the distractions away is our sacred word. While we don't chant the word, we use it to focus our heart on deep listening rather than the chattering. The word might be *God* or *love* or *home*. Some people use the word *surrender* or *open*. Whatever your sacred word might be, it's a sort of broom that sweeps away your thoughts or feelings for a later time of reflection. It's a windshield wiper. For now, all I'm doing is letting go. Entering the cloud of unknowing, availing myself of Mystery. Opening to nothing. Here comes a thought. "Surrender." And I let that thought float away. Oh! An emotion. "Surrender." I let it go. We should practice centering prayer daily for at least twenty uninterrupted minutes. Commit yourself to this practice for thirty days and see what begins to happen in your waking moments.

There are variations on the theme of centering prayer, and there is no one "right" way to practice deep listening. One option is the ancient practice of silently repeating a holy phrase while sitting in a contemplative posture. Traditionally, something like, "Lord Jesus Christ, have mercy upon me, a sinner." But it could be, "Be still and know that I am God" or "Come, Holy Spirit." Practitioners of this form of deep listening suggest that after a while, the words become embedded in one's heart in a way that all of life repeats the phrase. Richard Rohr uses Psalm 46:10 as an entryway into deep listening. He repeats it slowly, taking away one word each time: "Be still and know that I am God. Be still and know that I am. Be still and know that I. Be still and know that. Be still and know. Be still and. Be still. Be." Then comes twenty or thirty minutes of deep listening. Another form of deep listening is sitting in silence and focusing our attention on our breath. When our minds begin to run away, we simply return to our breath as it is life and connection. A sheer, untamable presence.

I tell my students to find what works for them. There is no right way to engage in deep listening, though there are unhelpful ways that engage our minds rather than quieting them. And sometimes it's almost impossible to sit in quiet because we are just too distracted or too tired or too whatever.

But it's the intention, not the outcome, that matters. We might remind ourselves that faith is always about the intention to be present and open to God more than it is about somehow being "right." As long as you are regularly practicing solitude, silence, and deep listening, you are on the contemplative path. You're becoming more fully the love that God has created you to be for the sake of healing and wholeness in the world.

Is Mindfulness the Same as Contemplation?

At the risk of splitting hairs, I think it's worthwhile to consider how practices of deep listening relate to what is called *mindfulness*. Mindfulness can be thought of as heightened attention in our waking moments that enables us to understand and experience the world with different eyes or "the mind of Christ." From the moment we are born, our brains begin to structure and categorize our world. Children are incredibly imaginative because the categories of experience and meaning-making are not yet fixed. But over time, our brains begin to sort and fix things into categories. We'll say more about this in chapter 4, when we talk about bias and cultural formation. But for now, we should understand that as we grow, we tend to become "mindless."

Harvard psychologist Ellen Langer describes *mindlessness* as "the rigid reliance on old categories."[24] When we are operating out of mindlessness, we "treat information as though it were *context*-free—true regardless of circumstances."[25] She goes on to explain that over time, people often operate as if their views of the world and its categories are fixed, and "we then tend to cling to these rules and the categories we construct from them, in a mindless manner."[26] Think about it. This is how most faith communities function. We learn categories and rules for our life together and begin to assume that's how our faith in Christ is supposed to be. We act as if Jesus himself gave them to us. "The rhythm of the familiar lulls us into mindlessness,"[27] and churches thrive on the familiar. Perhaps we should intentionally add something unfamiliar and unexpected in worship just to foster awareness and reflection. And maybe to see who responds with criticism such as "That's not how we do worship," which can open the door to conversation.

One of the important aspects of mindlessness for those who lead faith communities is its relationship to context: "Most people typically assume that other people's motives and intentions are the same as theirs, although the same behavior may have very different meanings."[28] Langer explains that we usually view other groups through our own cultural lenses without having a deeper understanding of the categories and meaning-making that exist within their cultures. In other words, our minds are constantly judging others against our own standards without recognizing that there might be other valid ways of living life and, for our purposes, life in God. This insight is extremely important for those who wish to lead with love. If we don't recognize that we're viewing things through our narrow experience, we'll never be able to love well. Mindlessness leads us to be judgmental and disapproving, even when we might claim to love everyone. As we'll see in subsequent chapters, the brain science is clear. It's not enough to simply announce, "I love everyone the same." You don't. I don't. But we can become increasingly aware of the categories we hold and the meaning created by the way we've been formed to live in the world.

Recognizing our tendency to be mindless is the first step toward becoming mindful. Mindfulness allows us to create *new* categories in our minds. Langer suggests that for adults, in the absence of "psychotherapy or a crisis as motivation, the past is rarely recategorized. We might from time to time call upon different episodes from the past to justify a present situation or grievance, but it rarely occurs to us to change the way events or impressions were initially stored."[29] Contemplative practice, though, can bring to our awareness categories, experiences, and ways we have been treated or mistreated, things we cherish and cling to or dislike intensely. It can show us our wounds and how our desires drive our actions. Deep listening helps us to see beyond the categories we've created and ask new questions. Deep listening, as it chips away at how we've been constructed and formed into a "self" that needs to be right or important or winning or rule-abiding or people-pleasing or whatever, enables us to carry that reformed self into relationships with others. We begin to "pay attention to the situation and context" mindfully.[30]

When we interact with the world, mindfulness reduces our defensiveness, it makes us open to new information, it enables us to see that there are multiple ways of experiencing and understanding the world, and it leads us to care more about good process than demanding certain outcomes.[31] It's as if the Spirit nudges us in our waking moments: "Can you see that? Look carefully!" If God created change and growth as a basic principle of life in the cosmos, then loving leadership requires us to care more about the process and the people than achieving any predetermined or expected outcome.

Our process often begins with conclusions that are held till death do us part. That's why we say someone is *married* to their ideas or practices. But faith can't be about certainty or closure or a closed mind or heart. When we create the church as a process that forms people into a rigid view of God, others, and the world, we've become closed off to the Spirit. It seems that Jesus kept pointing out that the processes being used to form people for life in God and community in first-century Israel were causing exclusions and harm and that maybe changing and making those processes less fixed and rigid would better express the love of God and neighbor. That's true for us today. And we have the gift of brain science to help us recognize that we are formed in communities that too often move toward excluding those who are different. More about this point later.

Deep listening makes us more aware of our wounds and constructed categories of being in the world. We grow increasingly conscious of our own stuff that gets in the way of loving and leading well. We become more open and less rigid. More thoughtful and less argumentative. We are gradually healed by the Spirit from the inside out. This makes us more mindful in our interactions with others and the natural world. So mindfulness probably shouldn't be equated with the practice of contemplation. Rather, mindfulness is a fruit of that practice carried into our lives. Deep listening is like stopping to fill the tank with gas, but mindfulness is driving down the road with an alert and perceptive awareness as if traveling to a place we haven't been before such that we can't travel on autopilot as we so often tend to do. Contemplation in silence and solitude shapes us for mindfulness in our noisy, busy world. Together, they form us in patterns of deep listening. Contemplation leading to mindfulness should remind us of Paul's claim to "pray without ceasing" (1 Thess. 5:17).

If we hope to lead with love rather than just claim to lead with love, deep listening is a crucial foundation on which to build our ministry. It sustains us. It reveals who we really are and who God calls us to be in this life. We might say that deep listening is the heart of our vocation or, perhaps, the breath enlivening our calling. We can't love God's people and world unless we are consistently connecting to the depths and listening to the Spirit. The intentionality with which we pursue our own spiritual development makes a difference. You can do church without deep listening. You can manage an organization without deep listening. But you can't do life in God without it. In today's world, we must set aside our sense of being too busy to be silent before God for twenty minutes each day. To think otherwise is a sure sign that our ego needs exactly that time apart. And if we aren't intentional about silence and contemplation, our daily lives are unlikely to stumble on it.

At this point, you might be thinking, "Sure, that's fine for me. But I'm never going to convince my community members to practice contemplation." Well, probably not immediately. Remember our discussion of McLaren's stages of faith and the need to grow our faith communities? Most Christians haven't been taught deep listening. Prayer is usually thought to be telling God what we want and need for ourselves or others. Loosening fixed practices of prayer can be a slow process of growing people spiritually, not unlike Moses leading God's people by stages in the wilderness. As leaders, the depths of our love will open others to trust our leadership. People might be curious about the calm, nonanxious, loving, peaceful presence they sense in us and want to know where it comes from. They might not initially be open to contemplative practices, but that's the direction we are leading.

We first teach them to question, even to doubt. We show them that Jesus told parables and stories to make us think more deeply and then think again. The Bible isn't a window into the past but a mirror in which we see ourselves reflected. We help the people see how cultural formation creates rigid categories. How mindless we become over time. We shake things up from time to time, knowing that disrupting the familiar becomes a portal to growth. And we keep loving and staying in relationship with each one of them, even or especially those who seem most critical of our leadership. Deep listening heals and makes whole. In that gift of God, our leadership of love for and among God's people will flourish. *Sola Spiritus.* Stay open to the Spirit and listen deeply.

Practice Makes (More but Not Completely) Perfect

1. If you don't engage in a regular contemplative practice, begin one. There are many apps available that can guide you. Try the "Centering Prayer" app by Contemplative Outreach. The "Sacred Space" app can guide you through *lectio Divina*. Or simply set a timer for twenty to thirty minutes once or twice a day and be still. Commit to the practice for at least thirty days. Don't give up if you miss some days. Just start again. Remember, it's about giving yourself fully to God and God's desire to love you into wholeness. Deep listening is our most important skill for ministry.
2. Preach and teach more often about the difference between religion or church and spirituality. One is the vehicle, and the other is the journey. They need each other, but the abundant life Jesus offers is found in the Spirit. Preach and teach about the way the world and our particular way of doing church form our brains in patterns and categories that aren't the only way to be faithful to Christ.
3. Quietly observe the way people in your faith community engage spiritual practices. Are they open to trying new ways of encountering God? Are their practices fixed and formulaic? (Do we always have to call God "Father" as if that's the "right" way to address the Holy Mystery? Do we always have to bow our heads when we pray? Can we only sing certain kinds of music or only from a certain era? Etc.)
3. Model for others the way of love that comes only from deep listening (contemplative practice leading to mindfulness) and its fruit in our lives. If we lead from the depths of the Spirit, others will follow.
4. How would you answer God's question to Elijah: "What are you doing here?"
5. What does *sola Spiritus* mean to you? How might it lead you beyond the walls (literally and metaphorically) of your heart and your faith community?

Resources for Going Deeper

Bourgeault, Cynthia. *The Wisdom Jesus.* Boulder, CO: Shambhala Publications, 2008.

Keating, Thomas. *Open Mind, Open Heart: The Contemplative Dimension of the Gospel.* New York: Continuum, 1997.

Nouwen, Henri. *The Way of the Heart*. First Ballantine Trade Paperback Edition: December 2003. New York: Ballantine Books, 1981.

Rohr, Richard. *Just This*. Albuquerque, NM: CAC Publishing, 2017.

Rolheiser, Ronald. *The Holy Longing: The Search for a Christian Spirituality*. New York: Doubleday, 1999.

Teresa of Avila. *The Interior Castle*. Translation and introduction by Mirabai Starr. New York: Penguin, 2003.

Thurman, Howard. *Disciplines of the Spirit*. Richmond, IN: Friends United Press, 1963.

⚜ 3 ⚜

CARING

Leadership Principle Four: Learn to love yourself so you can love others

WHEN I WAS a teenager, I rode the bus to my high school, a brand-new school in Littleton, Colorado, named Columbine. One day while riding the bus home, my friend Suzanne turned to me and said, "Elaine, you're always so deep in thought." Her comment caught me off guard. Wait. What? She was showing me something about myself that I wasn't yet aware of: other kids were talking and engaging one another on the bus, and I was looking out the window, lost in my thoughts. It was a bit of an awakening for me, obviously, since I still remember it decades later. There are always dimensions of our lives that others can see, but we have to learn about ourselves. Our interior world doesn't always neatly match the reality that lies beyond our minds.

One evening while in graduate school, I joined some friends for dinner at Armin's apartment. As we were cooking and talking, someone mentioned a school shooting at a place called Columbine. Of course, I was pulled back into memories from years earlier. As the news reporters discussed the layout of the school—where the cafeteria was—and mapped the tragedy, I could not reconcile my memories and maps of the school with what was being shown and discussed on television. What I knew to be true didn't seem to be. Later, I learned that the school had been remodeled at some point, so what I remembered could be true. Yet our memories and our experiences are partial and at times interwoven with other memories. Maybe I was also remembering my middle school and weaving it into my high school memories. In other words, our experiences are always interpreted by our brain and may or may not match the exterior world.

Often, church members point to a glorious past that ought to be recovered when, in reality, their memories are partial and biased. I may think I'm loving everyone. But other people might see in my actions and words clear evidence that that's simply not the case. We are more than our interior experiences, beliefs, and memories. In fact, if that's the basis out of which we operate, we have yet to learn the way of Jesus. We are also a complex biological organism. We are a body, mind, emotions, and spirit existing as this thing I call my *self*. And my *self* is never really a free-floating, separate entity but always connected to the whole of creation, though usually we don't see and acknowledge that interconnectedness. More on this in the chapters to follow.

In the last chapter, we considered how each human being, including those of us who are called to lead faith communities, has an interior, spiritual life and should spend time alone listening to God every day. Deep listening is a sure path to gradual healing and clarity. It is our most important skill for ministry. *Sola Spiritus*. In some ways, our spiritual health is the doorway to holistic well-being as it enables us to grasp who God has created us to be. We also began to think about how our human brains organize information as we grow, creating categories and adding valuative judgments to those categories (i.e., what we think is good and bad, right and wrong, better and worse), and then we mindlessly cling to them as *the* way of being in the world or *the* way of doing church. In the next chapter, we will examine our biases more carefully and what brain science teaches us about how we human beings create communities around such judgments.

But we first need to understand ourselves as individuals better than we do. We need to learn to love ourselves, our whole selves. That's our fourth leadership principle. We are self-contained bodies but not always self-aware. Others often see things about us that we are unable to grasp looking out from this body. Brain science begins to hold up a mirror that allows us to learn how to love more truly as we understand ourselves and others. We learn that leading with love is about caring for the whole person—body, mind, emotions, spirit—incarnate in a particular time, place, and multiple cultures. Brain science is a gift from God as it enables us to become more loving. Brain science doesn't teach us the gospel; it teaches us about God's creation, ourselves. I suspect that in the years ahead, brain science will profoundly change the way we do ministry. To love ourselves as God loves us, we need to care about the whole person, including our own body, mind, and emotions. And when we love ourselves properly, then, paradoxically, that love pulls us outward from ourselves. We are no longer snagged by our own stuff.

Have you ever been in conversation with someone who is wounded by an experience they've had in life, and that wound colors everything they do? Maybe they experienced a great tragedy like the sudden loss of a loved one. But sometimes it's simply that "someone done me wrong," and every interaction is shaped by that perceived injustice. The lens they use to view the world is a distorted one. Others can see they have a chip on their shoulder, but they're convinced it's just how things are in the world. They are so busy protecting their wounded heart that they end up hurting other people. Can love change their view? And what if the wounded one is called to pastoral ministry? Learning to see ourselves with the mind of Christ can lead us toward healing and wholeness so the wound becomes a sacred scar, and we can be a once-wounded healer.

We've talked about the "heart turned in upon itself," which is how some theologians have described sin. We probably need to rethink how we talk about sin as it too often has reflected cultural standards in labeling others who are different as *sinful*. This dehumanization of another person as being *more sinful* and, thus, less "fully human" has been leveled at women, people of color, those who have disabling conditions, gender-nonconforming persons, and members of the LGBTQ+ community, among others. Let's be clear though: this is a difficult subject. Suppose my culture values freedom, while another one sees obedience to authorities as more important. I might examine this difference and still conclude that my culture's value is preferable. But that doesn't automatically make the other way sinful. Sin is really a matter of causing harm, destroying goodness, undermining God's promises of life and love. In the New Testament, we translate *hamartia* from the Greek as "sin," but it really means "missing the mark." That's a good starting place. It reminds us that people often aren't trying to be harmful to others but that our good intentions often miss the mark.

Have you ever had a conversation with someone and you were trying to be helpful and kind, but the words struck them as hurtful? You didn't mean to offend. You missed the mark. We all "see in a mirror dimly" (1 Cor. 13:12), as Paul put it. We don't see through the mind of Christ. Confessing Jesus Christ doesn't suddenly make us healed and whole and fully loving, though it is the entryway or door or starting point for growing into the Christ character and love. It's an acknowledgment that my way isn't the best way to live, that I need to hear and respond to the way taught and lived by Jesus, who is the Christ. When I step onto the way of Jesus, my life is still missing the mark, but my aim is getting a little better. We come to see how our own hearts are turned in on themselves so that gradually over time, more of our interior lives turn outward to God and others in right relationship. The heart of the gospel is simply that we were once broken and separated, and now in Jesus Christ we are rightly related in love. We're becoming love as God is love as we let our wounds and selfishness be healed. Sure, sometimes people intentionally do harm. But for many of us, we think we are doing right, but we're not. We're just a little off target.

This insight is on full display in the story of the garden of Eden (Gen. 2:4b–3:24), though we often miss the mark on that story as well. Remember that the tree in the middle of the garden is the "tree of the knowledge of good and evil," from which they are prohibited to eat (Gen. 2:17). The woman and the man who was with her are later told that eating from the off-limits tree will make them "like God, knowing good and evil" (Gen. 3:6). The first sin isn't pride. It's the lie itself. The human problem begins with the lie that we can be "like God." Then we can deem others unworthy or unlovable or less than human. The lie is perpetuated from generation to generation in different forms.

Once they eat from the tree, their consciousness changes. They hide. They put on fig leaves—which, by the way, most people are allergic to. They are probably scratching themselves and are very uncomfortable; ancient peoples would likely be laughing at the story. In other words, the people now experience shame at their nakedness as if it were evil and make bad choices to fix a problem that didn't exist before they made it a problem. They now have categories of *good* and *evil*, but they clearly don't have perfect discernment about what is good and what is evil and how to determine which is which.

That ambiguity continues to be the reality of human life. Some folks think they know with certainty, but usually they are making a case for their side out of a dualistic way of seeing the world. What a fall from grace! Once we had the mind of Christ, and now we see in categories and dualisms. Life is ambiguous. The only thing we know for sure is that God is good and God is love and that our choices in life should further God's goodness and love in ways that build up the whole of creation to flourish. But we don't always know the good and loving choice or action.

So does this mean we are fatally flawed creatures, trapped in our sin? Is there "original sin" as a defect in our souls? Well, maybe. Then again, we were created in the image of God and declared to be "very good." It all depends on how you read Genesis chapters 2 and 3. Is the story of the garden of Eden simply about pride, disobedience, and punishment? Or is it a story about the human capacity and inevitability of growing in consciousness and agency, that is, choosing to live in ways that bind us together rather than divide and conquer? Is it about learning to "see" again in a way that doesn't divide and conquer but comes back into relationships?

Often our "sin" is inherited; our formation itself is missing the mark. We are taught that certain people are bad or dangerous or less human based on physical characteristics like skin color, size, age, gender, language, or sexuality. This "knowledge" is learned. It's not innate. A baby is free of categories. But then we are formed to hold categories mindlessly. The heart turns in on itself as it judges others to be less worthy or less human. This, again, is what I call the *sin of comparatives*: better than, worse than, more than, less than. We aren't taught by Jesus to make these judgments. In fact, Jesus is more likely to tell us to check out our own failings before we point our fingers at others. Too often we set ourselves up as the center and the standard for being human and are unaware that's what we're doing. Brain science also suggests that traumatic events we experience in life can, indeed, be transmitted from generation to generation.[1] And trauma creates wounds. Wounds often lead to the heart turning in on itself. Our wounds then lead us to wound others, like an injured animal lashing out. Or they lead us to believe the lies that others tell us, which is sometimes called *internalized oppression*. Our wounds prevent us from hearing and seeing. Our wounds say, "This reminds me of something that happened twenty years ago, so you must be bad too."

The basic human condition, then, is often less about "sin" as a power that makes us do bad things (sins of commission) or not do something we should (sins of omission) and more about the necessity for humans to listen deeply to God, to dismantle harmful categories we've learned, and to receive healing for ourselves, for others, and for the whole of God's creation. I'm not suggesting that humans can simply choose not to sin. We do need God's grace and forgiveness to change. We need God's love. We need the guidance of the Spirit. We have to be reformed across our lifetime, whenever we become aware that our formation is unwittingly dehumanizing others—or ourselves. It means, in a very real sense, confessing that the path of Jesus changes me from a selfish person who thinks too highly of my own way or too little of who I've been created to be into one who is more loving and rightly related to all of God's creation, including myself. I walk the way of Jesus that leads me to see myself and others as God does.

The way of Jesus teaches that I must first acknowledge and admit that I need to be healed of my own wounds, which contemplative practice and learning about my brain can help me to access, recognize, and release. Coming to see myself as I really am so I can begin to experience the goodness of our createdness usually takes some effort to rewire my brain from its habituated patterns. How do we begin to experience the world, in all its suffering and terror, as a place of possibility and love, where we are more likely to contribute to its goodness and healing than to do more harm? How can we inhabit the *basileia,* or reign, of God that has drawn near in Jesus? Let's say it begins with recognizing that the "mind of Christ" is not simply poured into us when we confess Jesus. Rather, we slowly grow into this God's-eye view over a lifetime of recognizing how our brains work to shape us in patterns that are limited and limiting. We can learn new ways of being in the world that lead us to love more deeply and truly.

Remember our discussion of Brian McLaren's stages of faith, how we might grow in our ability to see things more fully? That's the mind of Christ growing in us. We have to become increasingly aware of how our minds, bodies, and emotions shape us and our actions and beliefs. We have to move what's happening in our lower brain into our cortex so our actions become more thoughtful and intentional. That involves learning what we're clinging to in our hearts. Not surprisingly, love isn't simply a matter of our relationship to the Spirit. Salvation isn't just about our spirit. It's also about the healing of our minds, bodies, and emotions as part of that salvation we are offered in and through Jesus Christ.

We are created as incarnate, particular, embodied, culturally formed people. Healing isn't just about going to heaven when I leave those things behind. It's about becoming fully human, healed and whole, love incarnate in the time and place where I exist. It's about my full participation in the healing and wholeness of everyone and everything instead of doing harm to others and creation. Wherever I do ministry is the exact place where I am to be a conduit of God's love for the healing and wholeness of all people and the planet that is our common home.

An Interlude on Expanding Our Minds

Every practice of ministry—everything we do "on behalf of God," every *how* or *what*—has a why. Whether or not we're aware of what we're doing, there are reasons behind it. That's one of the things I emphasize with my seminary students. Until we think through why we are preaching or teaching or leading, our practice will be less effective than it might be. Why do I preach? Why do I lead the faith community? The answer, of course, is about God's work and mission in the world and enacting that faithfully. It's about contributing to the healing and wholeness of my faith community, my local community, the world, and the universe. Sometimes churches make survival their mission, or numerical growth, or staying just the way we are. That misses the mark.

I've told the leadership of my aging but otherwise healthy church that we need to change in ways that will be conducive to the spiritual growth of young adults, or I'll end up presiding at funerals for all the members. Either outcome can be in service to God, as long as we are focused not on ourselves but on God's mission in the world. We are called to be the body of Christ in the world, to channel love and healing to all of God's creation. We are followers who are supposed to be doing. Leadership is about faithful and hopeful attention to grow into God's promised future of love and justice so it draws near in a particular time and place. If my leadership isn't fostering and furthering God's desire for love and justice to reign, then my *why* is missing the mark.

There are times when the *why* is practical. Once when I was pastoring a small rural Georgia church, I asked if we could move the pulpit more toward the middle of the altar area since the Word is central to our worship experience. I was young in ministry and trying to think about the visuals of worship. They responded that they tried it once, and it didn't work. I asked, "Oh, why not?" I was about to launch into an explanation of the centrality of the sermon in our tradition and blah, blah, blah. But their answer stopped me. Apparently, the microphone cord wasn't long enough. And for me, in a small congregation with a limited budget, spending money on moving the pulpit wasn't practical. The *why* was not so much theological as practical. And that was just fine.

However, our *why* must always be grounded in love. Love is the heart of the gospel, the heart of ministry, and, frankly, the very nature of God. We are commanded to love God and neighbor as our primary work, and justice—right and equitable treatment of all—is part of love. I stand fast on the claim that if we don't first get love right, we'll not get the practice of the faith right. Insisting on beliefs and morality will never teach us to love. Only love cultivated and practiced can lead us to beliefs and moral positions that heal and make whole.

If you've read the book of Isaiah, you'll see that God is centrally concerned about justice as part of what it means to love the Lord your God and your neighbor as yourself. In the first thirty-nine chapters, we learn that the leaders in Jerusalem weren't concerned about justice. They were getting rich on the backs of those who were poor and ignoring the requirement to care for the widow, orphan, and stranger left without social and economic support to meet even basic needs, thanks to the human systems in place. The prophet warns them: You keep this up, the outcome of your actions won't be good. It's not God punishing them but their own choices, their failure to be loving and just, that eventually leads to exile. (They also choose to make an ill-considered alliance with the Egyptians, the place of their former captivity, but that's another story.) They were their own worst enemies.

So are we. When we fail to act justly and to love deeply, we end up doing harm, often justifying our actions in the name of God. Think of justice as the true justification for our actions: that everyone is treated in a way that builds up and enables them to flourish here and now. The religious authorities of Jesus's day were so busy upholding their beliefs that they could not see how they were excluding and harming women, children, strangers in their midst, those who had illnesses, and people who had jobs they didn't appreciate, like tax collectors. The religious authorities were so busy judging others that they didn't even see Jesus for who he really is. Jesus just kept showing them how to love rather than judge. He showed them that excluding only did harm. He tried to get them to see how to hit the target rather than miss the mark. "Your aim is off," said Jesus. "Here, aim in this direction." But they turned their bows and arrows on him. They would send him to the cross for loving those they excluded.

Unfortunately, too often we assume we are expressing love and justice when we aren't. And our actions have consequences for ourselves, for others, and for our planet. As Brian McLaren puts it, "People can't see what they can't see unless someone helps them see it."[2] Which, by the way, is exactly what Jesus tries to do in the first century and the twenty-first century. God wants us to see things more clearly, less dualistically, more relationally. Taking on the mind of Christ is about doing the hard work that helps us to see, hear, feel, smell, and taste more accurately over our lifetime. Our experience of God in the world will shape our brain and our beliefs. When we open ourselves to be shaped by God's love toward all, without the strings we so often attach, then our actions become loving and just. We stop being divisive. As McLaren so wisely suggests, "People who love do not need to agree."[3]

With this in mind, I want to offer a brief explanation of the theory undergirding this book. If you find it difficult or distracting, you can probably skip this section. But some of you will find that the theory at work in the background provides you with a bit of an a-ha moment. You'll come to see the importance of the skills we need for effective ministry in the twenty-first century. You'll realize that our minds are continually opened to seeing more clearly how the world and people work. We human beings are always growing as individuals and as a collective. Seeing as God sees is much more difficult and demanding than we normally realize.

Philosopher Ken Wilber's book *Integral Spirituality* is complex but insightful.[4] It utilizes a lot of terminology that is unfamiliar to most of us. It pulls together many philosophical approaches. But his basic sketch of human understanding helps us to grasp that in every situation, in every moment of leadership, in everything we do there are always four different dimensions of that experience or moment at work. There are four different perspectives or realities that are influencing how we understand what is happening. If we are unaware of any one of them, our grasp of that moment will fall short of the "mind of Christ," the big picture in which we get closer to seeing things as they really are. You can begin to grasp the implications for leadership. If we are seeing only from our own experience and perspective, we will be missing the mark and might just do harm.

Wilber posits that we have two individual perspectives and two communal perspectives. The individual and communal perspectives each have an interior and exterior dimension, so they can be modeled as four quadrants.[5] The interior of the individual is the "I" or the "subjective," where our experiences and our spirituality shape how we encounter the world and process anything that happens. Lots of people get stuck in this quadrant as what is "true." The exterior of the individual is the "objective," the "It," and relates especially to our brain, which is the seat of our physical and emotional well-being. Often, we are unaware of what's happening in our own body.

Brain science tells us that experiences, as raw sensory input, first enter our lower brain, the brain stem, which is often called the *reptilian* brain, and then proceed to our diencephalon, where experiences are stored and categories created. All inputs from the world that come via our senses are initially processed at these lower levels. Our diencephalon compares the current input to past experiences. So before we can really think about something using our cortex—the highest part of the brain—our lower brain has already caused us to feel and respond based on past learning and experiences that have been stored and categorized. If we've always heard that Black men are dangerous, then when we pass by a Black man on the street, we'll respond with fear.[6] We say we love everyone the same, but our lower brain is making judgments without having engaged the conscious, reflective part of the brain. In other words, we are programmed for bias toward others. We'll talk more about this later. But the implications here are clear: our brains are judging people and situations before we have a chance to really think about them. You can see how this might not be so helpful for someone who wants to be loving toward all.

So, then, each of us, pastors and church members alike, have the individual interior and the individual exterior going on. Pretty complicated, isn't it? We can't fully see ourselves, let alone the motivations and experiences that are driving those we lead. But we can be aware this is happening, and that's a huge starting point for leaders. We begin to recognize that there are many ways to understand what's going on. It gives us pause. And that pause may be exactly what my brain needs to activate the cortex and think more carefully. Maybe that's why Jesus so often asks questions or tells a story. Such things cause us to pause.

To make any situation or event even more complex, Wilber shows us that there are always two communal dimensions at play in how we understand and respond to experiences and situations: the "We" or communal interior ("intersubjective") and the "Its" or communal exterior ("interobjective"). Think about the communal interior as all the formative influences of the cultures to which you belong—and this is true of each person we lead. The church you grew up in has cultural norms. Your racial and ethnic identities provide cultural norms. There are norms arising from the region, country, city, or rural town that you grew up in. The health or dysfunction of your family growing up will create ways of responding to others and expectations for how we should think and act. These communal influences shape how we understand things because our communities, like our brains, are geared to make meaning of the world we inhabit. What and who are safe? What and who are dangerous? What and who are good? What does it mean to live a good life? Well, says each culture, let me tell you.

Language is a significant dimension of culture (even churches have a "language" that outsiders to the community won't know until they learn it). The first language we speak has a profound effect on our way of interpreting the world. If you're Inuit, you have dozens of words for snow.[7] If you speak English, it's all just snow, though it can become slush or be given an adjective like *crunchy* or *powdery*, unless you learned English as your first language in Fiji, and then what is snow at all? Which culture do you think understands snow more deeply or mindfully? Just because my culture says to do things one way doesn't mean it's the only way to do something. Without some intercultural awareness, including of my own communal norms, I can't be open to love others well. I'm much more likely to be judging their way of life, even if unconsciously and unintentionally. Even if I don't want to judge them. Simply because I've grown up in and been formed by these communities and not those, my mind will draw comparisons. We'll go into this intersubjective piece, the communal and cultural formation we experience, in the next chapter.

Finally, there is the complicating dimension of the communal exterior. Let's call it *context*. It's the thorn in our side at times because so often context is simply beyond our control. Whether we like it or not, it's shaping our leadership. A great example is the COVID-19 pandemic. There was nothing we could do to change the pandemic and mandates to stay home. Every church had to adapt or simply close and wait it out and see if people came back. The laws of the nation are a context we can't change; the same is true of our denominational rules or squabbles. We can choose civil disobedience as a response or take on justice activities to change the laws or rules, but the context remains. We can only be aware of it and respond to it. For faith communities, the larger context today is so complex: demographic shifts, spiritual but not religious populations, distrust of institutions, global migration, social media, climate change, racial injustice, gender fluidity, the pandemic, and more. Sure, it makes people want to go back to the way "things used to be" or "those good old days." Remember, though, that those days weren't so good for a lot of people. Jesus always invites us into God's future, where love and justice flourish.

Add to this larger perspective the immediate context of the neighborhood in which our faith community is planted. Are we in a neighborhood experiencing either decline or renewal? Is the neighborhood filled with children and schools or mostly senior citizens and assisted living facilities? Is the community wealthy or lower middle class? Do the people in the neighborhood look and speak like the ones inside our building? The immediate context is precisely the place where we are called to undertake the mission of God as the incarnate body of Christ.

And, yes, there's yet a third way to approach context: each faith community has its own internal context that needs to be examined. Perhaps our context is an aging building with too much deferred maintenance. Maybe our context is a worshipping community that has outgrown the space. Maybe we are financially strained. Perhaps we have a faith community eager to serve beyond the walls or one that is inwardly focused and not interested in serving the community. This interior context is the most malleable to change, but change is still not easily accomplished. In this sense, adaptive leadership provides helpful insights. We might hold on to Reinhold Niebuhr's prayer: "God grant me the serenity to accept the things I cannot change, courage to change the things I can, and the wisdom to know the difference." The

Serenity Prayer encapsulates the human journey of love and the need for each of us to take on the mind of Christ for the sake of the world. In chapter 5, we'll go deeper into contextual analysis and adaptive leadership as skills that can help us to see and facilitate change. Slow, measured change.

To lead well, then, we have to become aware of these different dimensions of each situation and community we are helping to lead. Where these four quadrants meet, we come closest to a God's-eye view of the situation, though it's impossible for human beings to have perfect understanding. That's part of the humility that comes with embracing our finitude. We are not God or Jesus. We aren't perfectly aligned with the Holy Spirit. We will always miss the mark, but we can learn to get closer to the bullseye. We'll be forced to make decisions about the priorities for our ministry on behalf of God in the world and then take slow, steady steps in that direction. Pastors today are often not equipped by their seminary education to understand all dimensions of what's happening in those situations we encounter in ministry. But if we seek to facilitate faithful and hopeful *attention* to grow into God's promised future of love and justice, then we must increase our awareness, which means growing into the mind of Christ or a way of perceiving that is wholistic. There is so much more to being attentive than meets the eye. Literally. But the more we learn to see, the more we become the love that by faith we hope to be.

Wrestling at the Jabbok

Let's think about the story of Jacob, who becomes Israel, the father of the twelve tribes that compose a deeply relational way of living. He starts out very self-focused and becomes somewhat more aware of the larger picture as the story unfolds. When Jacob is returning home to face the things he is and has done, he spends a night wrestling with an angel of God and comes away with a limp and a new name (Gen. 32:22–31). Jacob has to come to terms with his own self-interested behaviors, with the baggage he has carried and how it has harmed others for the sake of his own advancement. He is changed by his awareness and is given a new name, Israel, which means "let God prevail" or "wrestles with God." Only one who wrestles with God and lets God prevail can live in good and life-giving relationships.

He also most likely had to wrestle with the generational trauma passed down by his father, Isaac. Having Abraham almost kill him on a mountain wasn't a holy moment; it was traumatic. If Isaac was a real human being, this would certainly cause lasting woundedness that can be transmitted from generation to generation. The trauma is transmitted not so much through genetics but through the parent's unresolved experiences as they create emotional patterns in their children.[8] Maybe, too, he had to wrestle with what it means to be a man in his culture as he limps away, no longer bearing the same strong body that came to the river. Jacob is wounded in his body and his psyche. Whether the stories of Jacob are historical or mythical doesn't matter. The meaning is the same. Most of us are wounded or formed over time in ways that continue to influence our brain and our unconscious responses to others. We carry trauma from the past that sometimes triggers us to react in ways we'd rather not. But there are strategies for becoming aware of these wounds and automatic responses so that our relationships can grow more loving. Change is possible, but we have to wrestle with who we are so that we might become who God asks us to be. And woundedness doesn't mean God can't use us, though we must have the courage to wrestle at the Jabbok and come out of the encounter a different person.

The human creature is "fearfully and wonderfully made" (Ps. 139:14). We are created in the image of God (Gen. 1:26–27). We have all the makings of loving beings. God has lovingly created a world in which we can flourish, in which everyone and everything can flourish. It's a universe in which all things connect or work together for our good (Rom. 8:28). Once we acknowledge the goodness of the way things are woven together, we can begin to wrestle with God, let go of our expectations, and promote and preserve the relational web of goodness.

This relational perspective doesn't apply just to the orderliness of the universe; it also applies to each of us. Human beings are a complex composition that weaves together the physical, emotional, mental, and spiritual. We are organisms that need to find balance and right relationship within ourselves if we hope to be loving toward others. We all know that when we are sick physically, it affects our emotions, our intellect, and our spirit. If we are grieving, our body, mind, and spirit will suffer. All dimensions of our incarnate lives work together for our good. This means, as leaders, we need to take care of every aspect of the life that God has given to us. We need to promote the same in those we care for. If the last chapter focused on our spiritual development as central to growing in love, our starting point in this chapter is simply for each of us to ask: How well am I doing in body, mind, and emotions? Are these pieces of my humanity in right relationship and tended to? Am I encountering healing in mind, body, and emotions? If these are out of balance, our love will be too.

Here we'll start with just a few words about the physical health of clergy, recognizing that bodily health can't be isolated from the other dimensions of our being. Then we'll turn to emotional health and suggest that emotional intelligence is one of the most important skills we can develop for effective leadership amid conflict and division, as well as to lead the adaptive change we'll consider in chapter 5. Our wounds and past formation influence how we respond to others despite our claims that we love everyone the same. Often in the case of our bodies, minds, and emotions, we are not fully aware of how we are functioning. But there are ways to wrestle at the Jabbok if we are open and willing to be remade for the sake of God's work in the world. We might come away with a limp, but we'll be a better leader for it.

Fearfully and Wonderfully Made

Bill Bryson's book *The Body: A Guide for Occupants* is a wondrous journey through the mysteries of our bodies. Did you know "it takes 7 billion billion billion . . . atoms to make you," and "no one can say why those 7 billion billion billion have such an urgent desire to be you"?[9] We are all just atoms, lots of them. But they join together in a relationship that is unique to each of us. Did you know that a pair of lungs "smoothed out, would cover a tennis court, and the airways within them would stretch nearly from coast to coast"? And that stretching out "all your blood vessels would take you two and a half times around Earth"?[10] Just spend a couple minutes taking that in. Think about how much is packed into our rather unassuming bodies. And when Bryson places our DNA before us, he turns us into a universe: "if you formed all the DNA in your body into a single strand, it would stretch ten billion miles, to beyond Pluto. Think of it: there is enough of you to leave the solar system. You are in the most literal sense cosmic."[11] This cosmic "body is a universe of mystery. A very large part of what happens on and within it happens for reasons that we don't know."[12] Why do we have fingerprints? Why aren't any particular atoms in charge of our bodies? Why do "humans share 99.9 percent of their DNA, and yet no two humans are alike"?[13]

Ponder for a minute our breath, which biblically is pretty much the essence of life. Our breathing is truly mind-blowing. Imagine if we had to remember to breathe. How could we ever do anything else? Each year, we take about 7.3 million breaths, which adds up to "550 million or so over the course of a lifetime."[14] But here's the truly stunning fact, especially if we consider the idea that God has woven together every created thing: "Every time you breathe, you exhale some 2.5 sextillion (that's 2.5×10^{22}) molecules of oxygen—so many that with a day's breathing you will in all likelihood inhale at least one molecule from the breaths of every person who has ever lived. . . . At the atomic level, we are in a sense eternal."[15] We breathe molecules from Jesus's breath.

Are you falling in love with your body? It's all miraculous, mysterious, and marvelous. Talk about being fearfully and wonderfully made. Yet too often we take our relationship with our body for granted. We don't invest in this relationship, or we do so poorly. And the Great Commandment reminds us that to love our neighbor, we have to first love ourselves. The problem here, in part, is the modern dualism that separates mind from body.

Basically, modernity has told us the mind is important, the body not so much. The devaluing of the human body, over many centuries, has led to associating the body with the feminine, the earthy, the material world, all of which is too often deemed sinful. As Sallie McFague demonstrated in *The Body of God*, "Western culture and religion have a long, painful history of demeaning the female by identifying her with the body and with nature, while elevating the male by identifying him with reason and spirit."[16] This logic creates a dualism that suggests that men operate from their minds and women from their emotions. Men are strong; women are weak. Men are godly, women sinful. But who today could dispute the wonderful way in which God created our human bodies? Or that our mind is actually part of our body and connected to our emotions, which should all be animated by our spirit? What a sacred relational universe each body really is. How can we call sinful that which God deemed not just good but very good (Gen. 1:31)?

In the modern era, as reason took center stage, the mind became associated with men and the body with women, and the mind and men were valued over women. Today, that dualism often continues. At times it's blatant, as in those religious traditions that consider women unworthy of leading congregations based solely on their God-given bodies. And, yes, I know those traditions selectively use the Scriptures to defend their position. But what did Jesus say about women in leadership? And how did he relate to women and children? When he touched them, he wasn't made unclean and unworthy. Rather, they were declared whole.

At times, this dualism is subtler. A good example is found in the book *The Other Half of Church*, which suggests that our spirituality will be aided by reclaiming the right side of our brains, the part of our cortex that houses the emotions, relational capacities, the creative, the earthy, the compassionate, and tender.[17] The authors get a lot right in pointing to brain science and recovering the neglected half of our human brain to take on Christ's character more fully. They recognize the importance of community and relationship to human well-being. They emphasize love and joy. The authors are clear about the need to grow in awareness and maturity across a lifetime, and they present a developmental model to help embrace that growth. They even suggest contemplative practice, though they call it "quieting ourselves" through practices like "breathing, tapping our bodies, and yawning."[18]

But even as the authors highlight the problems of modernity and its overvaluation of the mind and "right thinking" as the truest expression of Christian faith,[19] they never acknowledge or even recognize the need to rebalance so-called masculine characteristics ("left brain") with feminine ones ("right brain") that have been rendered or categorized as superior and inferior human qualities. They don't recognize the wholistic, unified nature of the brain. Why do schools in financial difficulty cut programs in the arts first? Yet, often, sports remain. Both masculine and feminine traits are necessary to be fully human. If these authors, whose theology is more traditional, named the right half of the brain as the locus of what has been deemed feminine qualities, the implications for those Christians and their ministries would probably be rejected by their communities. So even though they clearly state that the problem of modernity is behind this dualism, they stop short of naming the feminine as an equal and vital aspect of every human being as created by God. We can't reclaim the feminine under masculine packaging.

These traits are not to be equated with identifying as male, female, or gender nonconforming. Jesus displayed both masculine and feminine traits, though we need to be careful about becoming too dualistic here. There are variations across a wide spectrum in joining masculine and feminine characteristics, although our language tends to obscure these differences. Remember, as a result of our formation in communities, our brains create categories of what it means to be a man or a woman and then assign certain characteristics. Dominant Western cultural frameworks tend to lean into these binary categories, though some cultures, such as many North American Indigenous communities, have always held three categories: male, female, and "two-spirit."[20] Think of phrases like *man up* or *stop being a sissy* when a man is displaying what is traditionally considered more feminine characteristics. Or calling a girl a *tomboy* if traditionally masculine traits are present.

But, again, Jesus displayed the full spectrum of human characteristics: courage and compassion, stoicism and emotion, strength and tenderness, reason and embodiment, a love of learning and a deep connection to nature, transcendence and immanence. If you think for a moment about Jesus's story, women play a prominent role in balancing the patriarchal values of his day: the story begins with a mother giving birth; in ministry, he welcomes women and "feminine" actions such as holding children; at the cross, the only ones who stay connected to him are the women "watching from a distance" (and, of course, John in the Gospel of the same name); and it's women who are the first witnesses to the resurrection.

Here's the interesting thing. We can't discuss this balancing act without language, and the language we have is already biased toward categories and how people "should" act according to the bodies they were assigned at birth. In learning language, we learn categories according to our community's values. Then leaders of faith communities are often expected to display certain characteristics that are more "masculine" than "feminine." This is a social and cultural overlay on the faith that needs to be rebalanced. The truest human being, revealed in Jesus of Nazareth, displays a healthy balance of human characteristics. It's how our brains have been created to function optimally. The authors of *The Other Half of Church* are right in claiming so. The balancing act is one of the most fully human things we can do. It's also one of the most sacred ways to honor the human body God created.

Mirabai Starr is an interspiritual writer and teacher who has studied mystics, and especially women mystics, across religious traditions. Unlike some scholars, she doesn't advocate dismantling patriarchy in favor of matriarchy; the goal isn't to replace one extreme with another. The goal, if we use McLaren's language, is harmony or oneness. We might even call it *radical relationship*, moving beyond rigid dualistic thinking. We need to find balance. To see more deeply. To become mindful rather than mindless. We need the mind of Christ. In contemplating the importance of God's creation and the healing of the earth, Starr embraces the healing power of the feminine: "Our global climate crisis demands that we break our habits of over-consumption and engage in voluntary simplicity. This is the antithesis of the dominant culture's emphasis on power through acquisition and the primacy of the individual. Yet it is the quintessence of the feminine values of cooperation and generosity. The masculine paradigm is predicated on scarcity, while the feminine is rooted in abundance for all."[21]

She then reiterates that we should not equate these values with the categories of *men* and *women*: "When I speak of the masculine and feminine values I do not mean the literal male and female. I am not blaming environmental degradation and economic injustice exclusively on men and suggesting women were neither materialistic or greedy. . . . Because both religion and politics, historically intermeshed, have been dominated by systems that empower men and oppress women, essential feminine values have been subverted, and this imbalance is reflected in the way we treat nature and one another."[22]

Starr's point is not to beat up on men. It's not to make anyone feel guilty. She turns to women mystics such as Julian of Norwich and Teresa of Avila to demonstrate, instead, how they "adore the presence of the sacred in all things. It's about celebrating life—food, sex, beauty—not denying life."[23]

The point here is to embrace the human body and the earth, "the body of God," in the words of theologian Sallie McFague. Remember that the sacraments represent not only the body and blood of Jesus given for us but also the "body" of God, who vivifies the creation. We aren't suggesting that God is equated with the created world, but God is the creative force at work in everything. God created the atomic and molecular structures of the creation and gives life to each particle of existence. The sacraments are an expression of all things being in radical relationship: God, one another, and gifts of the earth itself—water, wine, bread.[24] At heart, "the path of the feminine [is] the path of connection."[25] In fact, Starr illustrates how the feminine mystics point toward a "more egalitarian and relational," "horizontal, inclusive leadership."[26] Women mystics understand that contemplation of the divine isn't about escaping the world: "She turns inward, where she recognizes herself in all beings, which moves her to turn outward and act on behalf of the whole."[27] Simply put, "effective activism arises from unconditional love."[28] As Richard Rohr frequently explains, true contemplation leads not to "navel-gazing" but to action on behalf of a suffering world.[29]

The rebalancing of masculine and feminine traits for leadership in faith communities has no agenda other than the flourishing in love and justice of the universe that God created. Until we learn to embrace and honor the range of human characteristics within the bodies that we are given, our world, our societies, our churches, and our lives will be out of balance, lacking in harmony, unable to take on the Christ character in ourselves and our faith communities. We won't be agents of God's justice; we'll simply beat others up with our own positions and presumptions. And we won't see with the mind of Christ. Without the balance of our human characteristics, we can't express the fullness of interdependent, *agape* love.

Our Bodies Matter

If you've decided you're in love with the bodies God has created, then it's time to ask how you're caring for your own, as well as other bodies. It's probably not surprising that clergy health statistics suggest that many pastors aren't doing as well as we could be in caring for our own physical well-being. If we neglect our body, we aren't bearing faithful witness to the way of Christ. I'm not suggesting we never get sick or have to manage long-term illnesses. But are we doing the best we can with what we have?

How interesting that physics tells us matter can't be destroyed. The same matter that was in the beginning continues to be present today. We can destroy the form of something through our neglect or judgment or misuse, but the created substance belongs to God and remains, even eternally. This is what physicists call the Law of Conservation of Mass. The substance of creation cannot be destroyed by human hands, though we can do great harm to the way those atoms and molecules have miraculously and mysteriously come together in unique, irreplaceable, incarnate forms that God would have us honor and care for. Remarkably or ironically, "those people" detested by ancient Israel or your church today are literally part of you: same atoms, same breath, same created stuff. You are connected to each other by the very hand of God. You just don't usually see it.

Studies tend to focus on the mental health of pastors, which makes sense given the nature of the vocation. We seem to do worse at emotional well-being than we do at physical health, giving ourselves away until there's nothing left to give. But physical health is a contributing factor in clergy burnout. A sampling of 221 full-time Roman Catholic, Methodist, Lutheran, and Baptist clergy, published in 2019 (prior to the stressors of the pandemic), suggests that the number and variety of pastoral duties often result in chronic stress. Think about the different things we have to complete or attend to in a given week. In a larger church, the volume of needs can be overwhelming, even if there's a capable staff. In a smaller church, your duties can include things like mowing the lawn, changing lightbulbs, and printing the bulletins alongside preaching, worship, funerals, pastoral care, administrative tasks, teaching, outreach, and more. We've all had the experience of thinking we've got things organized or under control for the week, and then something unexpected requires our attention.

We become stressed. And chronic stress "can have harmful effects on physical and mental health. For example, chronic stress is associated with increased appetite, preference for comfort foods, and visceral fat accumulation, all which increases the risk of developing obesity."[30] Other health risks associated with stress include high blood pressure, diabetes, heart disease, and depression. In their survey of 221 clergy, over half were classified as obese, and the pastor's years in ministry was not a significant factor in obesity, though age was.[31] Such studies should lead us to reflect on the way we care for our bodies but shouldn't be taken as determinative. Who can deny that ministry, indeed, can be stressful, and if we aren't paying attention to our bodies, they might just fail us? But the body is truly the "temple of the Holy Spirit" (1 Cor. 6:19). It's the only vehicle we have for traveling this journey with God and others. The good news, however, is that as we age in ministry, our perceived stress usually decreases.[32]

The authors also note that "lifestyle behaviors may help to protect clergy from the harmful effects of occupational distress."[33] Exercise is shown to reduce the risk of disease and protect against anxiety and depression, but sitting at a desk for hours increases the risk.[34] Our bodies are meant to be moving. A body in motion stays in motion. We don't need to be spending hours in the gym; we just need to walk, to take the stairs, to spend thirty minutes on a treadmill, to play pickleball, to garden or mow the lawn, to take a yoga class, to engage in some form of physical activity that we enjoy. Our practices of deep listening, of connecting with God, are the starting point for lifelong ministry, but we also need to care for the unique, irreplaceable body that God has given us and declares to be "very good."

Of course, as you've probably noted in the study, our bodies and our emotions are connected. Stress can undermine our physical health, but it's even more likely to affect our emotional health. Depression and anxiety often arise from the chronic stress that comes with caring for others, especially when we don't attend to self-care. Exercise and eating right can help prevent or minimize those outcomes. But our emotional well-being proves to be a much more complex reality and an important aspect of effective leadership. So as we turn to our emotions, let's stop to ask: How well are you doing in caring for the unique relational universe of your body? Do you model for others loving your bodily self?

Our Emotional Well-Being

Our emotions are as complex and amazing as the cosmos of our physical form. There is so much we simply don't know about the magnificence of our brains and our emotional lives. But what brain scientists do know is that what happens to us throughout our lives, and most especially in the first months of life, can have long-term and unrecognized consequences. Our emotional responses are often controlled by lower levels of the brain, and it takes some work to get those automatic reactions into the cortex so we can see ourselves more fully. Our brains, reactions, and emotions can be changed or controlled, but not without paying attention. If we're mindless, our emotions will get the best of us. Sometimes our love is undermined by our lower brain reacting to perceived danger or past experiences, causing anger or fear to flash before we have a chance to think. So, first, let's consider how the brain and our emotions work; then we can think about more traumatic and less dramatic experiences and how they can form any human being and our emotions, whether pastors or those we lead.

Being called into ministry doesn't magically fix the emotional wounds, trauma, and reactivity we carry. Being called into ministry isn't an excuse to neglect our own emotional health, to pour ourselves out until we have nothing left. Sometimes the stresses of ministry intensify our unhealthy emotional behaviors. I once worked with a pastor whose emotions could become the center of the faith community's conflicts as he often needed to be affirmed and valued. Whatever wounds he carried became emotional flashpoints. If he received constructive criticism, he was being "shamed" by others. If he wasn't getting his way, he would inevitably claim he was being mistreated. If approached by a member of the church who questioned something, he would argue and become defensive. This pastor had so many gifts—he was smart, capable, and creative—but his emotional immaturity kept getting in the way of building healthy relationships and leading with love. We are called to learn and grow into a healthy emotional person who can lead with a compassionate, empathetic, nonanxious, nonreactive presence. If we can't see ourselves, we'll not see others either. Effective leadership in any organization depends on both our IQ and EQ, and emotional and relational intelligence can be developed. Caring for our own emotional well-being and that of others is a twenty-first-century pastoral skill of the first order.

It's important to understand how our brains shape our emotional life. Bruce Perry, physician and neuroscientist, simplifies the brain structure as an inverted triangle.[35] At the bottom is the brain stem, which receives information from our senses. Again, this is what we call the *reptilian brain* as it houses our fight-or-flight primitive survival instincts. After traveling through the brain stem, the sensory information then moves into the diencephalon, or what Perry describes as the place of regulation, though it can also dysregulate us: "If someone is stressed, angry, frustrated, or otherwise dysregulated, the incoming input will be short-circuited, leading to inefficient, distorted input to the cortex."[36] In other words, before our thinking and reflecting brain can consider the input, our lower brain has already compared the present situation with previous experiences that have been stored in our brain. It can trigger a response as if that old experience is happening now. Before we can ask ourselves, "Is this the same thing that happened before?" our lower brain has already called the shots.

As we move upward in the brain, the limbic region is the relational part of our brain that is just below the cortex, where our reasoning and reflecting capacity is located. The limbic is the source of our emotional life. But if we are dysregulated by the lower part of our brain, then "it is difficult to connect with another person, and without connection, there is minimal reasoning."[37] The relational dimension of human existence comes prior to our beliefs and moral prescriptions, both as children and adults. When Jesus says, "Truly I tell you, unless you change and become like children, you will never enter the kingdom of heaven" (Matt. 18:3), it's as if Jesus is reinforcing the Great Commandment. You have to start with love. That's how we've been created. That's how our brains work.

From a faith perspective, this science is fascinating. If we aren't rightly related to others, then we can't think correctly either. Our right relationships, relationships of love, precede our ability to formulate beliefs and judgments in our thinking mind. So often we begin with beliefs or orthodoxy. But we are actually commanded to begin with our emotional and relational life, our love. Call it *orthopathy*, or right emotions or feelings. Only when we have orthopathy can our orthodoxy be a truer understanding of the way of Christ, which then means our orthopraxy, or right action, can result. I'd put it this way: if we want to take on the mind of Christ and see things as God sees them, we have to learn to love God and others first. Which is precisely what Jesus commands.

Daniel Goleman's *Emotional Intelligence* was instrumental in developing the notion of emotional awareness as a key aspect of leadership. If brain science tells us anything, it's that our leadership depends on our emotional intelligence and our ability to self-regulate, as well as to read and manage the emotions of others. Without this emotional piece in place, all our ideas and plans for developing our faith community's understanding and mission will lack the necessary relational basis to motivate and encourage the people of God. According to David Kinnaman and Mark Matlock, the authors of *Faith for Exiles*, data show that "resilient disciples" are formed and sustained through "meaningful relationships."[38] If our emotional wounds get in the way of healthy relationships, it's difficult to lead with love, even if we want to do so. We'll get in the way of what our cortex wants to accomplish. Planning to grow and deepen our faith community requires healthy relationships. Planning to introduce doubt or help our people grow in their faith, hope, and love requires emotional regulation in us and in them. Adaptive leadership depends on emotional intelligence.

Goleman's understanding of emotional intelligence depends on this self-awareness. We might say that unless we wrestle with our self-concern—the heart turned in on itself because of the lower brain and its survival instincts—we won't come to the relational capacity that is the heart of the Christian faith. At the risk of oversimplifying Goleman and others, we can think of emotional intelligence as consisting of four competencies: "self-awareness, self-management, social awareness, and relationship management."[39] We can frame it in terms of two questions: Am I aware of my emotions and able to manage them? Am I aware of the emotions of others, especially my faith community, and able to respond appropriately and cultivate those relationships?

The stronger our capacity in each of the four competencies, the higher our emotional intelligence and the more likely we are to be filled with love and effective in leadership. After all, the people we lead and serve aren't employees, which makes our relational capacities even more important in leadership. Goleman goes so far as to call emotional intelligence our "master aptitude, a capacity that profoundly affects all other abilities, either facilitating or interfering with them."[40] When we lead with emotional intelligence, our self-awareness and empathy enable us to respond with love to others, no matter what their emotional state might be.

But what if we know we aren't as emotionally intelligent as we need to be? If it's our lower brain that's dysregulated, is there anything we can do to increase our ability to see and control our emotions? The answer is yes. But it takes effort and intentionality to accomplish. The key is to understand that "we very often have little or no control over *when* we are swept by emotion, nor over *what* emotion it will be. But we can have some say in *how long* an emotion will last."[41] We can learn to recognize certain emotions as they arise and then rein them in. We can learn to recognize a dysregulated emotion as it arises so it doesn't control us.

Much of our emotional life depends on our earliest relationships in our family of origin. As Goleman indicates, "The impact of parenting on emotional competence starts in the cradle."[42] In fact, according to Perry, research shows that even in the absence of language and cognition, babies know if they are being nurtured and cared for or neglected. Infants sense whether they are held in safe relationships. Some of our emotional responses have preconscious or at least prelinguistic roots: "The key to having many healthy relationships in your life is having only a few safe, stable and nurturing relationships in your first year."[43] Perry uses the language of the caregivers' responsiveness or "presence," which should prick the ears of everyone in ministry. Every person wants to feel as if they belong and matter, even newborn infants. There is evidence that they can sense the emotional climate in the family despite an immature cortex. So the human being's emotional health depends on relationships and belonging from birth to death.

So, too, the health of any organization, especially a faith community. Relationships and belonging are what make our faith communities thrive. If our earliest relationships weren't nurturing, belonging to communities that nurture us later in life can help to change our brain's responses. Think about adults who grew up in a dysfunctional household but intentionally do family life differently with their spouse and children. Or teenagers who come out as LGBTQ+ and are rejected by their families of origin but are nurtured in the supportive web of the gay or trans community. They can heal if there is a community that will love them. We can learn to love ourselves and others if we have the right environment. Here we can see why it's so devastating when a faith community doesn't create safe, nurturing relationships but instead feels like a place of judgment and rejection. Healing and wholeness—salvation—happen in loving, nurturing relationships.

Our experiences in life and, for that matter, in a community that should be nurturing us have consequences for our emotional responses. If childhood experiences are negative, hurtful, or unsafe, those experiences will be the lens through which we interpret new events, situations, and experiences. Been hurt, judged, or rejected by a church? That's what will be triggered whenever you encounter "church people." We respond in ways that are predictable based on what we've experienced in the past. We already have "tapes" or "databases" running that often don't read the situation or the person accurately but approach situations through the lens of the past. You can see how this might "hijack" our emotions, to use Goleman's terminology.[44]

But our brains can change. We can become aware of our reactions and learn to regulate them. Changing requires us to become attuned to those patterns of behavior in ourselves or in others. We learn to pay attention. Though deep and formative, our early experiences and even our most traumatic ones can be moved into our consciousness through what Perry refers to as "dissociation" or "dissociative reflection," which is essentially "mind-wandering. . . . We reflect on the past and imagine the future, making dissociative engagement a key part of daily life."[45] We use the cortex to think about different ways of being and responding.

But the most important factor if we want to grow in emotional intelligence and reform our patterns of response is a supportive and nurturing community. For pastors, especially, when so much of the work is caring for the deep needs of others, it's vital that we cultivate our own networks of support apart from our ministry setting. Our family, our friends, and, yes, clergy colleagues are vital to our well-being as we also need communities where we are the one cared for instead of being the caregiver. Colleagues or licensed therapists are often the only people with whom we can discuss difficult and confidential matters. Without a support system, our emotional health will suffer and so, too, our love.

Healing can and does happen in the context of being cared for in a safe, supportive community or a place where we feel we belong. If healing requires community, those who are spiritual but don't participate in communal life might, in fact, miss out on the present offer of salvation as the healing and wholeness Jesus insists has drawn near and can be inhabited now. This insight provides another perspective on the claim that salvation is located inside "the church" or the *ekklesia*: those called out of a broken world into a community of healing. If the faith community isn't a source of safe, caring relationships, if it doesn't contribute to healing our emotional wounds, if it instead adds to them, then we aren't the *ekklesia* of Jesus but simply another expression of the world's wounding and judgment, though justifying our behaviors in the name of God.

Both the community and the individual can and should examine their wounds and ask whether they are acting out of self-interest and the reactive lower brain or as other-concerned, reflective, compassionate people. As pastors, not only do we have to work on our own emotional health but we also need the skills to grow the emotional well-being of our faith community. We need emotional intelligence as a skill set that functions in our leadership and in every pastoral task we undertake. Your brain is telling you what Jesus said: Learn to love first and well; then everything else will fall into place. Learn to love yourself so you can love others.

Practice Makes (More but Not Completely) Perfect

1. How well do you think you are taking care of your body? Is there anything you might do to make slow and gradual improvements? Remember, if we try to make too many changes at once, nothing is likely to stick. So start slowly and do one thing for thirty days to make it a habit.

2. Ask someone you trust—and who will be honest with you—about your emotions. Do they think there are emotions that you sometimes don't manage well? Ask yourself if there are certain situations or people that seem to trigger responses. It may be helpful to meet with a counselor who can help you explore these emotions and how to manage them.

3. Spend some time thinking about your ministry setting and the emotions that seem to hold sway. How do they make you feel? Do you recognize patterns among your people (fear, exhaustion, conflict, hopelessness, kindness, welcome, etc.)? Ask how you might begin to manage the less productive emotions and build on the emotional strengths of the people you lead.

4. Is your faith community creating relationships that feel safe or unhealthy? Does everyone in the community feel they belong, or do they think there are some insiders and others who are outsiders? How do visitors experience the relationships present? How might you begin to develop a healthier relational capacity within your faith community?

Resources for Going Deeper

Goleman, Daniel. *Emotional Intelligence: Why It Can Matter More than IQ.* New York: Bantam Books, 1995, and a new introduction, 2020.

Kinnaman, David, and Mark Matlock. *Faith for Exiles: Five Ways for a New Generation to Follow Jesus in Digital Babylon.* Grand Rapids, MI: Baker Books, 2019.

McLaren, Brian. *Why Don't They Get It? Overcoming Bias in Others (and Yourself).* E-book, 2019, www.brianmclaren.net/store/.

Perry, Bruce D., and Oprah Winfrey. *What Happened to You? Conversations on Trauma, Resilience, and Healing.* New York: Flatiron Books, 2021.

⟨ 4 ⟩

CONNECTING

**Leadership Principle Five: Learn to
see through your neighbor's eyes**

I'D BEEN SERVING my faith community, the Village, for about a year when I
got a visit from Pastor Girma and a member of his flock. Having migrated
to the city from Ethiopia, Pastor Girma led a small faith community that
worshipped in Amharic, the official language of Ethiopia, and had outgrown
the living room where they had been gathering on Sunday. I welcomed
them into our building, where they began to meet in our Fellowship Hall. A
month or two later, we were also approached by Germain, pastor of a nondenominational French-speaking Congolese congregation. Suddenly, we had
three different ethnic and religious cultures worshipping in our building.

On occasion, I would hear from one of my church members that the
Ethiopian or Congolese congregation was letting its children "run wild in
the building." I wondered if maybe they had a different cultural understanding at work. Did they view the building as a village (ironically, we call ourselves the Village) and all of us as a community that would care for their
children? Maybe in their home country, the church was the safest place their
kids could be. In our denomination, though, we have clear guidelines on
keeping children safe, and those couldn't be ignored either. We had to work
together as three communities with different values and perspectives to come
to agreements on how to keep the children safe. It was a lesson in intercultural communication—and a lesson we continue to work on years later.

Acting with love is our goal, but sometimes our cultural cues and
norms lead us into judgment. We don't understand people who are different.
We tend to hold our own way as the "right" way and then expect others to do
what we do. Usually, we don't even see what we're doing. But our communities are increasingly global and diverse, which means we can no longer live in

a way that avoids or suppresses difference. Appreciating other cultures and learning about one another's cultural values will be increasingly important in the twenty-first century if we hope to lead with love. We need to develop intercultural capacities, including learning to see our own cultural formation at work.

When we recognize that God has created all things in radical relationship, the leadership principle that presents itself is learning to see through the eyes of others. Our calling is to live with compassion into our human connections. We are called to inhabit those preexisting relationships God has already put into place, though we don't always see and embrace them, while respecting differences. Love builds bridges; it doesn't divide. And it never does harm to others based on different ways of living. Even if you consider someone's way to be unjust or unholy, denouncing or excluding them will never lead to love.

Every Human Being Is Biased

In the last chapter, we considered how our brains work. Experiences enter our brain stem, with its fight-or-flight response, and are lodged in our diencephalon, which is the source of regulation or dysregulation. Our diencephalon is basically the region of comparison as new experiences are evaluated against prior ones. And our limbic region houses our relational capacity, which responds before our cortex has a chance to think. Relationships can create a safe place for us to heal and be made whole. When we become aware of how our brain is functioning, we can begin to change our responses. We can begin to see the patterns into which we have been formed. To develop healthy physical, emotional, and relational behaviors, we have to create new patterns in the deepest recesses of our brains. Yet there's a catch: our brains are wired for bias.

When we hear that word *bias*, we think of prejudice. Situations that are biased are unfair toward some people. Bias resonates with injustice, and that can certainly be the outcome. And where there is injustice, love cannot flourish. But not all bias is unfair and unjust. I'm biased toward dark chocolate over milk chocolate, which you might consider a great error in judgment but you aren't likely to launch a movement in protest. You see, my brain is wired to create categories and think *this,* not *that.* If someone puts a box of chocolate candies in front of me, I've already limited my choices. *This.* When I go into a restaurant, the menu is already smaller because of my bias toward certain foods. Not *that.*

From birth, our brains sort and categorize our experiences. Perry explains that an infant's developing brain begins to "make sense of their world" by categorizing and organizing information such that they "make 'memories' of the smells, sounds, and images of 'our people.'"[1] We are relational creatures from our first breath and are formed in communities. As Perry puts it, "These memories exist on a very deep, pre-cortical, unconscious level: the way your people talk, the way they dress, the color of their skin."[2] *This,* not *that.* Anything new and different might be a threat to survival. When we are nurtured in healthy relationships, the familiar feels safe, and the unfamiliar leads to stress and dysregulation.[3]

Now we begin to get a sense of this concept of unconscious or implicit bias. Every human being is formed in communities, beginning as an infant who has no language yet and few categories in the brain. This process is simply normal human development. Remember, we are created by God to grow and learn. If we want to use the language of original sin, it might simply be wired into our brain as this dualistic propensity to prefer what we consider to be "my way" of life. Before that tree in the middle of the garden of Eden, we saw things holistically, with God walking beside us in the cool of the evening. But now we see in categories. And categories lead to judgment. Our wiring to prefer our own way is precisely what gets in the way of love. Our hearts and minds turn in on themselves.

Those categories continue to be shaped by experiences across our lifetime, adding to the process of *this,* not *that.* We learn how to make sense of our world and how we are expected to live within it. By mere chance of birth, I am formed in one family and community and not another. I become accustomed to certain ways of thinking, seeing, doing, behaving. I'm raised in this fundamentalist church and not in that progressive one. My faith is Baptist, not Lutheran, so I find liturgy strange and uncomfortable. My Anglicanism is formed in Kenya, not England. *This,* not *that.*

Jessica Nordell summarizes how our brains work from an early age: "Categorizing—turning raw sensory data into meaningful information by grouping things that belong together—allows humans to perceive the world, make predictions about it, and survive as a species. If a lion appears on the veldt, you have to know to run, but first you have to correctly identify it as a lion and not your grandmother. Categories are essential."[4] As we learn these categories and the ones that make us safe and help us to belong, we become *mindless*. We don't recognize the cultural formation of our brains. Nordell explains, "What lays the foundation for prejudice, it seems, is not the perceptible differences between people, but how much the culture tells us these differences matter."[5] Before our brains mature, while the cortex is still developing, they have been formed in a way that tells us to prefer "our people" over others. My way feels safe and right. That is what cultural formation does, and it's inescapable. To be human is to be shaped to live and participate in specific communities and to make judgments about which people are safe and good and which might not be.

It probably doesn't take much consideration to see how this kind of bias can eventually undermine our ministry. Let's say you have mental pathways that don't much like people who are overweight. In grade school, you were chubby and teased by the other children. The culture, crude as it was, said, "Being chubby is bad." You were picked last for every game in PE and not invited to birthday parties. When you had a growth spurt in middle school, you began to thin out, and in high school, you were a decent athlete. Something in your lower brain remembers being teased and says, "Overweight people are bad." Without even realizing it, you'll be more judgmental toward those folks and react to them in less loving and compassionate ways, even if those responses are almost imperceptible. Your lower brain is responding before you think about it. In other words, saying that "I love everyone the same" isn't how our brains function. Remember, our cortex is the last part of the brain to weigh in.

When we become adults, this categorizing often becomes subtler and more sophisticated as relational networks, media, and technology make "the categories erected in childhood fill to the brim with more and more cultural debris."[6] Our brains "tend to search for information that confirms stereotypes and ignore information that contradicts it."[7] For instance, if we were raised to think of scientists as male, when television or advertising shows us a male scientist, our brains will reinforce the idea that scientists are men, not women. We begin to shape the world in a way that says women aren't supposed to be scientists and see the evidence all around us. This is known as *confirmation bias*. We contribute to those messages, often unconsciously, and steer girls away from the sciences. In a similar way, we reinforce messages that say women aren't supposed to be leaders or in ministry. But these are culturally created categories, not God-given. People will search the Bible to confirm their cultural categories and biases. That's how slaveholders could justify their evil, death-dealing system. They found verses that "confirmed" their culturally created categories.

Such stereotypes, according to Nordell, "persist in part because they are culturally useful: they legitimize the status quo."[8] If the status quo is positioned in a way that enables and upholds privilege for some over others, you often can't see what's happening: "Privileges—with regard to gender identity, sexual orientation, race, ethnicity, or beyond—can create a sort of blindness to others' suffering."[9] At this point, bias does become unjust. We turn cultural formation into *the way things are* and refuse to see that it's a product of cultural formation, not God's command. We do harm because our categories have labeled and judged some difference among human beings as unworthy or less than fully human. We serve ourselves, not God and others.

You can begin to see that as the leader of a faith community, you're not simply dealing with beliefs at the level of your rational brain. Our brain unconsciously sustains and maintains the power of *this*, not *that*. We might think we are upholding God's way, but it's equally as likely we are upholding communal patterns that are based on the judgment of our communities about who and what represents safe, good, and "like us." Remember that those people in the garden of Eden were duped into thinking that knowing the categories of good and evil would make them "like God." Prior to eating of the tree, they didn't have dualistic categories. All things were rightly related and worthy of God. Everything was connected without the judgments that we've called the sin of comparisons. But eating from the tree created categories that reinforce exactly those places where we humans aren't at all "like God." The sin of eating from the tree of the knowledge of good and evil is thinking that we now are "like God" and can determine what is good and what is evil. But human beings see through a glass dimly. We see in a foggy mirror that is often only reflecting ourselves.

Let's say, then, you were raised in a town that was mostly white or mostly Latinx or mostly Black. As a child, you only encountered people of your own race: family, teachers, cashiers, babysitters. Those patterns of "safe" people are imprinted on your lower brain. While there are always some people who are explicitly racist, most of us don't realize the way "otherness" is being processed by our brains. Perry explains, "One of the hardest things to grasp about implicit bias and racism is that your beliefs and values do not always drive your behavior. These beliefs and values are stored in the highest, most complex part of your brain—the cortex. But other parts of your brain can make associations—distorted, inaccurate, racist associations. The same person can have very sincere anti-racist beliefs but still have implicit biases that result in racist comments or actions."[10]

When well-meaning people say, "I love everyone the same" or "I don't see color" or "I don't have a racist bone in my body," it simply isn't true. That's not how our brains work. In fact, "research shows that . . . belief in one's own objectivity and 'blindness' to gender and color . . . actually make bias worse."[11] We insist on our own way rather than opening ourselves with humility to accept who we really are. But the way of Jesus offers us hope. We can become more loving, accepting, and just. Science demonstrates that paying attention to differences and our tendency to stereotype, rather than insisting we are "blind," is essential to learning this *and* that.[12] The difference between living mindlessly and mindfully becomes a key skill for leading with love that connects us in healthy, life-giving relationships.

Paying Attention and Learning to See

We are brought back to our discussion of deep listening and the way it enables a more mindful engagement with the whole of God's creation. We've been given spiritual practices that, if we are open to the Spirit, enable our brains to change, to see, and to live into different patterns. Healing our bias requires spiritual practice that forms us in love. If we begin with beliefs and moral prescriptions and cling to them as "right" and "required," all they'll do is drive us right back into the rigid categories and patterns that Jesus tried to show us are harmful. But learning to listen deeply, to pay attention, to hear and see what Jesus is teaching and the radical relationships God has created enable the flourishing of love. That log in your eye? Maybe it's the categories made by human communities to make us "think" some people are good and others are bad. But we are not really thinking at all. We're on autopilot. We are missing the mark. But we can learn to adjust our aim.

Attention, deep listening, and mindfulness are practices of the Spirit that can facilitate rewiring our brains and overcoming our unconscious bias, at least to the extent possible in this life. Isn't it interesting that science tells us that prayer in the form of contemplation, quieting our incessant thinking and feeling to listen to God, can actually open us to love others more compassionately and deeply? Deep listening can move us beyond dualistic thinking to a more wholistic way of seeing the world, which we know to be "the mind of Christ." These disciplines "allow us to notice our thoughts, feelings, and behaviors as they arise. Practicing non-judgment helps us sit with those thoughts and feelings rather than turn away, even if they're unpleasant. And practicing attention strengthens our cognitive control, so we can have more influence over our reactions."[13] We can break those patterns that were formed in us by human beings. We can create new pathways that follow the way of Christ and are genuinely more just and loving.

"I once was blind, but now I see" takes on new meaning. Loving others requires that we learn to see in new, less dualistic ways. It begins with simply asking, "Am I seeing through my own eyes, my own experiences, and my own understanding of God and judging everything against my human formation? Learning to see as God sees begins with questions, which Jesus employed often as a strategy to open someone's eyes. "The challenge of addressing implicit bias," writes Perry, "is first recognizing that you have it."[14] Coming to consciousness, learning to see ourselves and others with the mind of Christ, is the goal. Moving from *this*, not *that* toward a place of this *and* that is the way of love when it comes to our attitudes and behaviors and connections to people who are different from us.

Remember, difference is literally only a fraction of our DNA: we are genetically 99.9 percent the same. And yet that fraction of difference accounts for the incredible diversity of human, and even planetary, life. When we begin to see our common nature and that we are all created in the image of God, then we can begin to embrace not only human diversity but also the biodiversity of our planet as the very fabric of our life. We are woven together for the good of all that God has created. There is nothing God has created that is not good, though we so often misuse and destroy that goodness. All things work together for good for those who love God and neighbor as themselves (Rom. 8:28).

So, then, if our brains are wired for bias, what hope is there for our leadership and our faith communities to love as God loves, unconditionally and infinitely, and in indivisible God-given *agape* relationships? Research shows us that there are some things we can do to reduce our own bias and help others grow in their openness to connect across differences. Years ago, as a young Air Force officer stationed in Korea, I had flown to Bangkok for a few days of vacation. On my return to Seoul, I made my way to the train station and bought a ticket south to the city of Iri, near the air base. Unbeknownst to me, that day was one of the most important Korean holidays, and the train station was jam packed. I stood frozen near the ticket window, unable to see anything but tens of thousands of people. Surrounded by difference, not speaking the language, I have no doubt now that my lower brain was dysregulated and stressed. These were not "my people." Sensing my bewilderment, a lady trotted over to me and pointed at my ticket. As I showed it to her, she grabbed my suitcase and started weaving through the crowd, waving for me to follow. I did. A few minutes later, she dropped my bag at a train platform, pointed, and said, "Iri! Iri!" Then she disappeared back into the crowd. I could only call after her, "*Kamsamnida*! Thank you!" Now I had an experience that could begin to change the categories in my brain. This kind woman had made me safe.

Years later, as a doctoral student in theology, I was selected to participate in a Church World Service (CWS) trip to visit refugee camps in Africa with the intent of returning to the United States as an advocate for how we might help the problem of forced migration. My team of four—three participants and a staff member from CWS—flew to Abidjan, Ivory Coast. The day before we traveled up country along the border of Liberia, during briefings at the US embassy, I passed out and was taken to the hospital in Abidjan (much later to discover it was a reaction to the antimalaria drug I was taking). The other three members of my team left the next morning, and I was directed to stay alone in the hotel until they returned since no medical help would be available near the refugee camps.

After a miserable day or two alone in the hotel, wondering if I would live through this experience, I got a call from our contact person with the United Nations High Commission on Refugees, a Jamaican lawyer. She recommended I change my ticket and take the Friday flight home instead of waiting for the others and leaving on Tuesday. So I asked at the front desk for directions to the Sabena Airlines office and then launched out from the hotel at midday into the heat of the bustling city of Abidjan. Two blocks to the right. Turn left at the bank and follow the street about three or four blocks. I had arrived at what seemed like one of the busiest intersections in the city. There was no ticket office in sight. I stood frozen as cars flew past. Then, seeing a tall young man talking to an older woman nearby, I walked over and, speaking almost no French, announced, "*Perdon.* Sabena?" They both looked at me. Then at each other. Then the young man exclaimed, "Sabena! Sabena!" He spoke to the woman in French and took off across the busy intersection, motioning for me to follow. I did.

Some minutes later, as we were traveling farther from the hotel, I came to my senses. My cortex began to function and asked, "What are you doing? You're following a complete stranger deep into a city you don't know, and you're not well. Maybe you better stop and get a taxi." Just then, as my cortex began its processing, the young man turned to me and said, "You speak English, don't you?" He went on to tell me he was a seminary student studying to be a priest. We spent the next ten minutes discussing Saint Augustine's theology until we arrived at the airline office. He waited while I changed the ticket and then walked me safely back to the hotel. For years after, Fr. Marius and I exchanged occasional letters. This experience of being helped by a stranger in a strange country also began to change the categories of *this,* not *that* to ones of this *and* that. This kind man had made me safe.

The first thing to recognize is that our connections to others are one of the most important avenues to reshaping our biases. We need experiences that challenge our categories. When we open ourselves or—to be honest, in the stories above—are forced due to circumstances beyond our control to rely on the kindness of strangers whom our lower brains might associate with being a threat, we begin to see anew. Had I not been in difficult situations, my brain would have kept me at a distance from the people who helped. Connections build connections. Experiences literally can change our minds about people. The gospel is premised on the idea that we will create new connections or, better, we will learn to see the relationships that already exist and set aside our own standards and judgments rather than imposing them on others. Perry puts it simply: "Create new associations; have new experiences."[15] We can learn how, when, and where those implicit biases begin to show up. We can spend time with people who are different. We can reflect on our tendencies without becoming defensive. We can love ourselves and love God and others enough to grow. We can cast out fear of the "other." Together, we are safe.

Nordell helps us to move beyond our dualistic formation. She demonstrates that "the urge to categorize is universal, [but] the perimeters of categories are not. How any community defines group boundaries and who belongs within them is changeable, and wholly specific to its time and place."[16] And, of course, our minds do change over time as individuals and collectively as human beings. It seems Jesus was always trying to help us see and unlearn categories. An unclean woman is touched by Jesus. A Samaritan turns out to be the one who knows how to love. A tax collector's home is a fine place to eat a meal. A leper is made well and no longer the "other" to be avoided as unsafe. It doesn't take much to recognize that categories are changing in our society, especially among younger people. For many, *male* and *female* isn't how they understand the world. Their brains are being formed to see and embrace more permeable categories (which doesn't, by the way, suggest that they don't have bias. Think about those Boomer memes). Perhaps our faith community, when we unconsciously uphold categories that aren't "status quo" to younger people, genuinely feels out of touch, unable to see or hear. It doesn't at all feel like a place of love but one of judgment.

We can do better. We can begin to see how we have been formed and create more permeable categories or ways of being in the world. Ways taught by Jesus. Ways that live into the goodness of the radical relationship that was present in the beginning. Ways that recognize that my fear is undermining my love. Perhaps you are beginning to grasp the importance of intercultural skills or the possibility of becoming less rigid in our cultural categories. This doesn't mean we become relativists for whom "anything goes." Rather, we become people who love first and foremost. Only love makes us safe, even though othering offers the illusion of safety. You can't judge someone into healing, but love can provide the safe space to grow and change together.

This leads us to examine the leadership of bridge-building, or making visible the connections that exist among peoples and all of creation. We are called to grow in our appreciation of other cultures and our ability to behave in ways that respect and uphold their humanity. Remember, we can't build a bridge unless we can see both sides of the river. We might not always agree with their cultural norms. But we are commanded to love, to uphold their humanity, to build up and not tear down. All are created in the image of God, a holy *"And"* that enables us to unite our categories of *this,* not *that.* Creator, redeemer, *and* sustainer. Fully God *and* fully human. Death *and* resurrection. Jew *and* gentile. The image of God is the holy *And* dwelling within us. It's the God-given connection point, but it can't function to give life abundantly unless we're aware of the cultural debris erected on top of it. The image of God in each person is the place where our cultural categories are pulled into love and respect for the differences God has created.

Building Bridges Everywhere

In Genesis 11, we find the story of the Tower of Babel. While some might view this story as demonstrating the pervasiveness of human sin—the desire to be "like God"—we also realize it's an etiological tale. It's intended to show why different cultures exist. When a child would ask why there are different languages and peoples, the answer for these ancient, premodern peoples was, "Let me tell you a story about the Tower of Babel." It was meant to be an explanation. It was intended to make sense of their world. It explained to premodern minds why different cultures exist.

In some ways, though, the story does point us to the problem of *this,* not *that* as it begins with the people thinking, based on dualistic categories of us and God, that they are perfectly capable of building their lives without God. Instead of being radically related to God, the people—at least those in power—decide they can be their own gods: We can be "like God" in our judgments. We are right in reaching toward the heavens with the tower we've constructed. And, in most societies, whoever is in charge calls the shots and insists on the sameness of the people. Maybe as the tower crumbled, so, too, did the illusion of sameness based on language and cultural norms. Oneness is only found when we are open to God and listening deeply.

Those towers we build to protect and privilege "our way" cannot lead us to God or love. They only divide us or, at least, reveal our differences. Across our lives, if we are following Jesus rather than reaching to the heavens and constructing the world according to our "safe" place, we will learn what the gospel teaches: We are all children of the living God, fearfully and wonderfully made and radically related in the web of creation. Made of the very same atoms and molecules. Dust to dust. Those atoms and molecules come together and are expressed in variations and hues. But we can't see the goodness of those differences until we stop trying to build up ourselves and our way as the only way that leads to or looks like God. We can't find unity without relationship to God that changes our minds about things.

Isn't that what the story of Pentecost in Acts 2 teaches or reveals to us? The disciples were gathered together in one place and engaged in deep listening before God. They remained open and waited until God was ready to act among them and show them something new. Then the spirit of God did an astonishing thing: they could understand one another while speaking their own languages. No one was forced into someone else's cultural reality, but they could now understand one another and live together as one people. The differences don't disappear at Pentecost. They aren't frowned on and squelched. They aren't judged, at least by those who receive the Spirit since, in Acts 2:13, those who aren't open and don't receive the Spirit end up judging. But to those who are open to the Spirit, differences become a remarkable gift of mutual upbuilding.

The Pentecost story demonstrates that the *ekklesia* of Jesus is intended to be a place of unity where we recognize and appreciate, even understand and adapt to, our cultural differences. It's how a faith community is meant to live. We come to understand one another and listen to each other's "language" without judgment. Pentecost is the ultimate story of bridge-building as the Spirit reveals the web of relationships that exists among peoples. We are woven together by God at the molecular level, though we find our vision obscured by the cultural formations that appear to separate us. Life in the Spirit should enable us to embrace and adapt to the differences that exist, to value them, and to break down the categories of *this,* not *that.* "Those people" are us, and we are "those people." And there is only one God, Creator of all. The Great *And*. The story of Pentecost, the birth of the *ekklesia*, suggests to us that we are not a faith community unless we can live into this interconnectedness as the way of Jesus Christ. We are not a faith community unless our hearts, minds, and actions reflect the unity of Pentecost. Yet Sunday morning continues to be among the most divided and monocultural spaces, an indication of our failure to truly understand what God reveals and enables at Pentecost.

Let's be honest. The church, as an institution, cannot express perfect unity. We are divided by our finitude. Geography, time, and language groups do, in fact, cause the formation of different local bodies worshipping Christ. Let's call that *context*, something we'll explore in the next chapter. We embrace specificity as the incarnation of the Word, the sacred, the holy. In fact, the only real body of Christ is the local one fulfilling the mission of God in the place it's planted. The *ekklesia* that Jesus anticipates is a spiritual reality visibly incarnate in particularity, in time and space and among people who live together in close proximity. We only become the body of Christ when the Word takes on flesh among us. The *ekklesia* is more than an idea; it's a flesh-and-blood ingathering of God's people as the body of Christ in a particular time and place. What binds these incarnate expressions together is the outpouring of the Spirit. The image of God, the holy *And*, comes alive as if connective tissue or a new neural pathway.

But we human beings, who so often miss the mark, have imposed social constructions and categories such as race and gender on God's people, making differences into categories for judging worthiness/unworthiness, superiority/inferiority, inclusion/exclusion. When we don't recognize the categories that form us, we reinforce unholy patterns. We demand that our beliefs be enforced and upheld. We haven't taken on the mind of Christ and learned how to love. We turn the church into a place of *this* not *that*, excluding others based upon the categories we've created. When we can't see beyond our dualisms, when we don't grow and develop spiritually, we find ourselves dehumanizing others. We judge and divide. We label other people as unworthy of God or as too sinful to be part of God's Church. We declare "Unclean" and send them away.

But who among us can accurately weigh "righteousness" or "sinfulness" on a scale constructed by God? Whom did Jesus label as "unclean"? The sin of comparisons is one of the subtlest and most destructive forms of human hubris. When we don't recognize that human categorization has been central to the institutional church and its failures, we find ourselves trying to build a tower to be like God rather than letting the Spirit miraculously and astonishingly unite us. In spite of ourselves. Our cultural formation turns the church into a place consisting of walls intended to keep people out. A fortress to keep "us" safe and "them" away. But the Spirit simply says: let people come together in their differences. The Spirit says, "Open yourselves and watch the connections grow." The Spirit reminds us that we are commanded to love, and whatever judgment may come belongs to God.

Remember how bias works in our brains: "To form categories is to be human, yet our unique cultures play a role in determining what categories we create in our minds, what we place in them, and how we label them. A fair-skinned person could be considered white in Brazil but Black in the United States. People from Japan and China are lumped together as Asian in the United States but seen as distinctly different elsewhere."[17] We are the ones categorizing as we try to make sense of the world, relying on human constructs. These categories aren't of God. They are ours, and we need to own them. We label our categories as God-given, but our minds and hearts are turned in on themselves, missing the mark. We are not created to divide and separate people according to our cultural categories but to see and live into the radical relationships that God has created. Perhaps one of the greatest spiritual gifts is to recognize that Pentecost is not supposed to reside *inside* the walls of "our church." Those first disciples weren't in a church when the Spirit rained down on them. Pentecost—bridge-building—happens everywhere if we can just learn to see with the mind of Christ.

One telling example of our propensity to miss the mark and reinforce homogeneity is the fairly recent premise of the church-growth movement known as the *homogenous unit principle*.[18] First articulated by Donald McGavran, this principle claims that to bring people to Christ or to plant churches, evidence suggests that commonalities among the people such as ethnicity, language, and culture will serve to grow the congregation's numbers. Today, brain science tells us that McGavran's principle stirs up and reinforces the category of "our people," who look and act like "us" and "our way." (Granted, it is an improvement over missionaries insisting that Indigenous peoples take on Western culture to follow Christ.) But it's hard to follow Jesus's way when we're insisting on cultural categories. McGavran and his church-growth followers emphasize cultural categories in the belief that more people will be brought to Christ. Increase numbers by reinforcing *this*, not *that*. But when we understand how the brain works, we should be suspicious of any principle that claims the gospel is best served by separating people into distinct categories of *this*, not *that*. Are we creating communities made in our own image rather than God's? Is separating people the way of Jesus?

This homogenous unit principle might, in fact, work well in forming a stage-one faith—simplicity, per Brian McLaren's analysis. But knowing that human beings are created to grow and develop, the homogeneous unit principle, at the very least, requires an accompanying principle and plan to move beyond cultural similarity to bridge-building. Stage-one faith lacks the kind of doubt that enables people to grow beyond cultural categories. Creating connections and deeper relationships among God's people is the essence of the way of love. That's being a neighbor. Being brought to Christ is about relationships and new connections, not further separation. The heart of the gospel message is that we were once separated and divided, but through Jesus Christ, we are again in right relationship to God and others. Homogeneity reinforces our human constructions and simply misses the mark of the gospel. It reinforces biased human categories.

We might even suggest that pursuing homogeneity reifies our human failings, sets them in stone in our minds and even our hearts as "God's way" when these are cultural and human constructs and categories. In biblical Greek, it leads to *xenophobia*, fear of the other, instead of *philoxenia*, which we translate as "hospitality" but literally means "love of the stranger or other." Demanding "our way" of following Jesus leads to conflict and division. Homogeneous churches almost never transition into multiethnic or intercultural ones.

The world is simply a more intercultural place than ever before thanks to technologies that allow for mobility and visibility. We see the world with our own eyes, and we move rather effortlessly from place to place. The physical barriers of the past have come down. Will we grow into the possibilities that are present when the world is knocking at our door? Or will we choose to bar the doors to the church and hunker down inside? Clearly, if the faith community's leadership is stuck in homogeneous cultural patterns as the right way, it will be difficult for that faith community to grow in its bridge-building on behalf of Jesus. We aren't called simply to "convert" *those* people; we, too, must be converted to the way of love across our lifetime and dismantle the categories that separate and divide us. This *and* that is our calling in Christ. So, Pastor, what is your plan to grow your people to see the image of God in each and all of us as the Great *And*?

The way of Jesus Christ, the way of love, is open to diverse expressions as sustained by the Spirit and, in a sense, judged by God, not by human beings. Only unconditional, infinite love can heal divisions. The Scriptures are clear that *agape* is about coming together as one people who embrace diverse tongues and nations and ways of living—not to change their culture but to embrace them in the love that leads to life. We, ourselves, will never be whole unless we are in relationship with whomever we deem "other." To baptize in the name of the Triune God (Matt. 28:19) is to set aside "my way" and become radically interrelated, dwelling in the holy *And*, which is God's very self. Baptism into the interrelated God known in three insep-arable "categories" represents letting go of the ego-driven demands of our human minds and opening ourselves to the healing and ingathering of the one God, who is pure love and relationship. Relationships have a mystery to them that can never be legislated into existence.

The basic idea here is that by grace, we're gathered into the minis-try of reconciliation, to the reality of connectedness, to the commitment to God's way, not "our way," to this *and* that. The one baptizing is not better or truer or more human or even godlier than the one being bap-tized. It takes humility to realize that God is always the agent or actor; we are merely a conduit for God and should get out of "my way" and let God's reconciliation and love bring us together into a place of mutuality. It means we learn from one another, and we are all changed in the process. Too many Christians throughout history have baptized in the name of "my way" only to do great harm rather than to heal and make whole. Salvation, the healing, wholeness, and reconciliation offered by God alone, can never be a weapon used by human beings for oppression and exclusion. If it's presented and inhabited as a way of judging or threatening others, it's simply not salvation.

When we consider Jesus's interactions with diverse peoples, it's clear he dismantled the barriers between people rather than seeking homogeneity. He changed the idea that our way is good and their way is bad to a third way: the way of love in which all of us are linked together for good in and through God's love for the whole of creation and each human being. "We know that all things work together for good for those who love God" (Rom. 8:28). Together. The reign of God draws near whenever we extend love and interconnectedness in the name of God. We move from seeing and experiencing the world in a dualistic pattern to one that is reconciled, and we can see such oneness only through the mind of Christ. God's way proclaims that we are all in this together, like it or not. It takes the log out of our own eye so we can see as Jesus does. Monocultural life breeds fear. Fear breeds judgment. Judgment breeds division. Division breeds conflict. Conflict breeds discord, hatred, even violence. It tears down. It is the antithesis of Jesus Christ. But the gospel always proclaims: fear not. It announces: peace be with you. The gospel always brings together and furthers life.

Intercultural life inhabits and visibly expresses the radical relationships that are part and parcel of the cosmos and the very nature of God, who has chosen to reveal the divine reality as inseparably three in one. We who are created are all made of the very same dust, atoms, and molecules. We who are many are also one. My breath contains the breath of every human being. My breath contains molecules once breathed by Jesus himself. The breath of our God, who is known as a Trinity, literally dwells within each of us. The breath of God upholds the life of everything. The calling of every faith community is to further this radically related life in the creating, reconciling, and sustaining Mystery. We are to love and serve everything created by God, making visible the already present relational nature of God's way. Being truly countercultural isn't about creating another human culture called *the church*. It's about living into the reconciling, indivisible mystery of God as the Great *And* that makes us one.

So, then, leave judgment to God. When we cross from this life to the next one, Jesus will not ask us, "Whom have you judged in my name? Whom have you pointed fingers at or called sinners in my name? Whom did you declare unworthy of me? Whom did you keep out of my body?" Quite the contrary, the only thing we will be asked is "Whom have you loved in my name? Whom have you visited, cared for, fed, lifted up, given life to in my name?" How have you woven together, reconciled *this*, not *that*, such that this *and* that is made visible? How have you baptized not into your dualistic thinking but into the three that are One and can never be separated? Love cannot exist apart from relationship. The only thing God has commanded of us is to love God and love neighbor in the same way we love ourselves. The three become one. Reconciled. Unified. Rightly related. If we don't get love right, our brains will continue to judge and dehumanize others.

Perhaps it is most telling that following Jesus's ascension, the apostles Paul and Peter are sent to the gentiles, even against their better judgment and contrary to their long-held categories. There's no denying that Peter is revulsed by eating "unclean" animals (Acts 10). Or that Paul discovers just how inadequately he has understood the truth of God, which is connection and reconciliation, not separation and division. They've spent a lifetime in "our way" and thinking in categories of *this*, not *that*. Paul is changed by the Spirit on the road to Damascus, but then he is "converted" again. First, Paul is transformed from a faithful follower of God through the law to a faithful Jesus follower and then to a faithful apostle to the gentiles, but he is still on the journey of growing in faith. It's as if he's moving through those stages of faith toward harmony. Simply confessing Jesus isn't enough to lead with love. It requires becoming open to and connecting with everyone, no matter their cultural norms. Paul continues to grow across his lifetime in ministry and in his understanding of who God is and what God asks.

Just as Paul goes through stages of conversion, so we also grow through stages of faithfulness. Each time the scales fall from our eyes, our minds conform a bit more fully to the mind of Christ. As we see with a new depth of understanding, God transforms us again and again. Once firmly in *this*, not *that* thinking—so firmly as to kill in the name of our way—now Paul's mind takes on the mind of Christ more fully, and he begins to see radical relationship and reconciliation as God's goal. He realizes it's pretty much the gospel in a nutshell. This *and* that becomes Paul's mantra: "There is no longer Jew or Greek, there is no longer slave or free, there is no longer male or female; for all of you are one in Christ Jesus" (Gal. 3:28). No longer separating according to dualistic categories but seeing everything as one in Christ, woven together, reconciled. Paul no longer seeks to destroy difference but in fact is willing to give his life to embrace it. Paul shows us the depths of bridge-building and how intercultural competence is one of the most important pastoral skills we can ever develop. Paul learns to be countercultural only when he begins to let go of his cultural categories and appreciate the differences.

Developing Intercultural Awareness

The first step in developing the skill of intercultural competence, or bridge-building, as an important attribute of the mind of Christ—as a spiritual discipline—is to learn about my own culture and see that each and all of us exist within these socially constructed ways of living. It might be helpful here to pause and define this term *culture* rather than assume it's self-evident. Cultures are often compared with an iceberg. What we see plainly is only the tip of the iceberg, and so much of our cultural formation lies beneath the surface, which is what tends to trip us up in our well-meaning interactions with those who are different. Culture, in its most basic definition, relates to the behaviors, standards, language, worldview, and customs of any group of people. How has our way of living together in a particular time and place been structured and organized?

Our way of being together is not the fullness of life together but one expression among a group of people. We embrace incarnation, but that which is created must always grow and change and learn. We must always keep moving toward resurrection, which means we'll have to lay down our "life" to get there. We form cultures with norms and expectations to make meaning of our world and, hopefully, to live with some common principles that connect us. A culture, though, is always a human construct that is both good and misses the mark in various ways.

Each and all of us live within multiple cultures. The community of faith in which I am raised forms me in particular cultural patterns. The region where I grow up teaches me specific cultural ways of life. If I play a sport and belong to a team, that, too, will serve as a kind of cultural formation. So will a fraternity or sorority. Those of us who served in the military understand that when we join up, we are formed into a way of living with its own standards, worldview, customs, and even language. In the US Air

Force, I had an AFSC, which in the army or navy would be an MOS. For the uninitiated, that's simply a way of talking about my military job. What college or university did you go to? Which customs were part of its traditions, and what did the rival school do that was different from your way of being together? Even my family of origin has cultural patterns at work, norms and expectations for how to live together. In many different ways across our lifetime, we are formed in cultural patterns, often without recognizing their influence on how we see and navigate the world.

Most significant, of course, are larger cultural forms such as national and ethnic groupings, often with distinct languages. Language is one of the most profound ways of shaping human categories, understanding, and behavior. In the United States, we are largely monolinguistic and often think everyone should speak English, which isn't consistent with the message of God at Pentecost. We can't understand or love others if we are unwilling to accept that our cultures have formed us to view the world in different ways, to value different things such as individual freedom or communal adherence, and that language is central to communicating values and expectations.

We can even see how language is behind and reinforces divisions in churches: What are the words we use to name God? What words do we use to speak about people? Are we "high church" or "low church"? Traditional or modern or contemporary? Evangelical or mainline? Catholic or Protestant or Orthodox? You can begin to see the way our language creates categories of *this*, not *that*. We then repeat these to our children and each other as if they are the right way to speak about the gospel, often without deeper examination. We get stuck in our categories and refuse to grow into the mind of Christ. Our lack of growth in faith and wisdom continues to divide us. Learning about our own culture and about other cultures without moving toward judging who is right is a first step toward seeing from God's perspective. Spiritual practice helps us to stop categorizing and start listening. Asking questions is the way of Jesus himself. Asking questions cultivates the mind of Christ.

Here, a word about *whiteness* and white cultural formation in the United States is probably helpful. Because the majority and dominant culture in the United States has been white over the last three or four centuries, it has often been "invisible" to those who fit into this category. When you are the powerholder, you expect that others will assimilate into your cultural norms and uphold the status quo that makes you comfortable. When you control the categories, you can decide who and what belongs and who and what doesn't. This means those in the majority don't really need to be aware of their own culture or way of doing things. They simply assume it is the right way for people to live. *Whiteness* is a social construct, and over the centuries, many people have either "become white," such as the Irish and many Latinx people, or "passed" as white due to the lightness of their skin. Race is a construction in which categories of *this*, not *that* are implanted in the brain. Add power for some over others into the mix, and it's a recipe for dehumanization. These are not immutable, God-given categories. They are cultural, social constructions. They are human categories.

Once we understand how our brains work and the categories we create, it's easy to see how people of faith can think of themselves as loving people when, in reality, they are doing harm to those who are different. Are we aware of the ways we might be reinforcing our own cultural standards as "simply the way things are?" A naïve and egregious example is the idea that we can teach our children about the gospel by showing them beads of different colors and attaching meaning to those colors. The white bead is goodness, godliness, righteousness. The black bead is sin and evil. "But aren't they just colors?" someone raises in defense.[19] For a child who doesn't yet think abstractly, we have just reinforced socially constructed categories of race in a way that says, "Being white is good; being Black is bad." Here is a "Black" person or a "white" person, and the child's mind fits them into those categories. Then suppose the family is walking around a mall. The child picks up on subtle cues such as the way Daddy greets white people but doesn't say anything to people of color. Or that Mommy clutches her purse closer whenever a Black man walks by. The parents are likely unaware of these behaviors since it's not the cortex or thinking brain at work but lower regions reacting to sensory stimuli. The child picks up on the cues, and they reinforce the categories of *this*, not *that*. Again, this process is what we call *confirmation bias*. We find things that confirm the categories we already have in place. But when we become aware of our own cultural conditioning, then we can begin to address those subtle, reflexive biases that we don't intend to perpetuate.

Learning about other cultures is like anything else we learn in this life on earth: it is a developmental process that stretches across a lifetime. It's helpful to frame our intercultural growth in terms of stages, though being careful not to make these categories too rigid or fixed. In fact, one need not begin at the first or even the second stage but can be formed as a child into a more advanced level of cultural awareness as, for example, in bilingual homes. One of the most prominent theories of how we learn to accept and adapt to different cultures is known as the Intercultural Development Continuum based on Milton Bennett's developmental model of intercultural sensitivity (DMIS).[20] Basically, the left side of the continuum—simply a line reflecting how we respond to cultural difference—is ethnocentric or monocultural ("my way"), and growth toward the right side of the continuum leads us into ethno-relativism or greater intercultural competence (the bridge-building of reconciliation and relationship).

Bennett's theory, developed by Mitch Hammer and others into a valid and reliable instrument for assessing cultural awareness, identifies five stages along this developmental line.[21] The first stage is *denial*, in which we either don't care about or are uninterested in thinking about any other way of living than our own. At this stage, I'm probably not even aware of culture or refuse to engage it. I have no interest in how other people might live. The second stage is commonly referred to as *polarization*, or the idea that many monocultural perspectives are framed in the dualistic mode of "us versus them" or what we have talked about as *this*, not *that*. You'll recognize a lot of polarized people in our country and in our churches: my way is right, and your way is wrong. Bennett also notes that a different form of polarization can happen, for instance, when college students study abroad for a semester. At times, they'll reverse the pattern and see their own culture as bad and the other one as good. Either way, the categories are dualistic rather than appreciating what might be valuable in both cultures or grasping that they relate to different worldviews. Here, I'm not really asking any questions about others who are different. I already know "they" are wrong; they aren't "my people." Polarization tends toward superficial understanding, and until we begin to see what people hold in common, we remain dualistic in our approach. As leaders, if we recognize that we or the members of our faith community are in a polarized mindset, then emphasizing our shared humanity—that we are all created in the image of God, beloved of God, made of the same stuff—is where we need to begin. We help them grow by first moving them toward seeing how we are the same in many ways.

The transitional developmental stage from monocultural to intercultural capacity is known as *minimization*. In minimization, we learn to appreciate cultural differences, yet in doing so, we emphasize sameness or similarities and minimize or become "blind" to important differences. As such, our own culture remains the standard, and we often assume everyone else is just like us. We assume everyone values the same things we do, reacts in the same ways we would react, and so on. Cultural differences remain largely hidden to us. We'll see the tip of the iceberg when it comes to cultural formation, but we won't see those deeper aspects. For example, a teacher who has always lived in the United States might view a Korean or Taiwanese student as quiet and withdrawn in the classroom. US students are often eager to raise their hands unless they're shy. But what if the Asian student's cultural formation taught them that students are to respond only when called on by the teacher, which is a sign of respect? My minimizing perspective has assumed we are all the same, perhaps to the harm of the student sitting before me.

I'm pretty sure most of our faith communities are at a place of minimization, at best, since most people who take the Intercultural Development Inventory are in this stage of minimizing differences. We claim to "love everyone the same." Yet when a person from a different culture enters our faith community, they quickly recognize behaviors that suggest that we don't accept differences. Maybe the visitor is used to shouting, "Amen!" in worship, but now people turn and stare when they do. Maybe the people respond to the visitor with microaggressions such as scooting away from them on the pew or forcing a smile or touching their hair as if to offer a compliment. When we can only see the similarities, we are able to love only what is like us and comfortable.

Minimization is considered a long developmental stage. It takes a lot of learning and experiencing other cultures to move from appreciating the ways we are all the same—a vitally important development in our thinking—to a place where we see and appreciate differences among cultures and can adapt our behavior when in other cultural settings. We have to learn to ask a lot of questions. How have I been taught to be polite or respectful? How do my people express anger? What's the "right" way to disagree? And do other cultures have the same answers as I do? We question our own human categories, much like Jesus's strategy of asking questions and challenging cultural norms to illuminate that they weren't created by God but by human beings.

When we transition beyond minimization, our intercultural capacity is now at the stage of acceptance. No longer needing to judge other cultures against my own, often unrecognized way of living, I can now see other cultures more fully and appreciate the differences. I now see that other cultures show respect or engage conflict in ways that differ from what I've been taught. I don't judge or ignore those differences. I'm not afraid of differences. And finally, as I grow in my ability to both see and adapt my own behavior when in various cultural settings, I move into the final stage of adaptation. I haven't fully arrived because I can never learn about every culture that exists. But I have developed a tool kit that enables me to listen and learn and engage other cultures on their own terms. My categories are more flexible and permeable than earlier in my development. I don't have to judge everything against my own experience but begin to see those cultures as their own way of being a community, even if at times I find some of their cultural practices harmful or not life-giving. No doubt they would say the same of mine.

The story of the Samaritan who is the "good" person on the road from Jerusalem to Jericho helps us think about these stages of cultural awareness and being awakened (Luke 10:25–37). Remember, the story is preceded by a conversation about the Great Commandment to love God and neighbor. Then the teacher of the law "who wanted to justify himself" (v. 29) asks Jesus, "Who is my neighbor?" That's when Jesus tells this story we know as the parable of the Good Samaritan. For the people of Israel, they would expect Jesus to tell them about the bad Samaritan, as those were the cultural categories at work among first-century Jews. The people of Samaria were reviled by Jews and vice versa. There was a long history of conflict between them. But instead, Jesus says both the priest and the Levite (in the *good* category for the hearers) pass by the man who has been beaten and robbed. Why? Probably because their culture tells them the man might be dead and is unclean. So, of course, they had to pass by. It was the "right" thing to do.

After all, they couldn't serve the community if they were unclean, and they were important men.

The Samaritan, who would have been disliked by the hearers of Jesus's story as "bad" or a "threat," is the one to show compassion, empathy, kindness, and love to the injured man. How shocking to the hearers! Jesus is demonstrating that different cultures can be as kind and loving as our own. They can be *more* loving and relational than our own. He shows us that cultural norms can do harm to others because they cause us to treat people as unworthy of our help (the injured man) or as someone we shouldn't be in relationship with (the Samaritan). Instead, Jesus invites us to open ourselves to the way the Spirit connects us as one people despite and amid our cultural differences so that we might learn to love, to offer healing and wholeness.

Another fascinating story about Jesus and bridge-building is the one of the Syro-Phoenician (Mark 7:24–30), or Canaanite woman (Matt. 15:21–28). As a woman, a gentile, and a foreigner, she is clearly culturally different from the disciples. The disciples have cultural categories and a mindset in place about how they should interact with or avoid *that* person. If we aren't interculturally aware, we'll read the story as Jesus reinforcing cultural categories of *this,* not *that.* Generally, we focus on Jesus and find his behavior a bit perplexing or use it as a defense of exclusion. But maybe the story is about whether the disciples have learned what Jesus has been teaching them. It's the pop quiz. It's the test that concludes Jesus's lesson on difference. Are they learning to see this *and* that?

To understand Jesus's encounter with this Canaanite woman, it's necessary to engage the larger context of Matthew 15. In verses 1–9, the lesson begins with Jesus pointing out that the Pharisees do harm in the name of upholding cultural norms associated with their construal of the law: "For the sake of your tradition [i.e., culture], you make void the word of God" (15:6). God gives the guidelines of the Ten Commandments, but the cultural system creates specific laws that can uphold love or dehumanize and do harm. They honor God "with their lips, but their hearts are far" from God, "teaching their human precepts as doctrines" (15:8, which draws from Isaiah 29:13). And those specifics often serve the powerful, those who can insist on their own cultural standards as "God's" way.

Then Jesus calls together the crowd that is following him and teaches everyone about what "defiles" (15:10–20). He tells them not to worry about what they put into their mouth (human categories of *clean* and *unclean*) but to beware of what comes out of their mouth—which either builds up or tears down others (15:11). Is God's way, or are my own categories, coming out of my mouth? The disciples, concerned that Jesus has offended the religious authorities, pull him aside. But he continues the lesson by suggesting that the Pharisees are "blind" guides leading the blind, "and if one blind person guides another, both will fall into a pit" (15:14). Those in power cannot see, other than their own self-perpetuating categories. Their hearts and minds are turned in on themselves, upholding their cultural way that is doing harm to many. They are more concerned with the rules they've established than they are with whether other people are suffering or flourishing. If those laws are good for me, what does it matter if they harm others?

Jesus tells his disciples and the crowd that the "leaders" are leading the people nowhere. Don't miss this point. When they cannot see their own cultural formation and the way it serves their interests while doing harm to others, the leaders will stumble and fall. They aren't hearing Jesus at all. They do not have the mind of Christ. They do not understand God's way. Their religion is just that: a system without spiritual depth, disconnected from the love of God and neighbor, which is the only law required by Jesus. The religious authorities teach beliefs that do not lead people along the way of God. When the disciples ask Jesus for a direct explanation of the parable, he simply points to the heart (Matt. 15:18–19). Jesus offers love, not adherence to a list of rules, as the way of God.

Now we arrive at the story of the Canaanite woman (Matt. 15:21–28). What seems remarkable and should give us pause is that Jesus takes the disciples north to "the district of Tyre and Sidon" (15:21). This is Canaanite territory, later part of Phoenicia, and in Jesus's time, these are Roman port cities. Today, this region would be in Lebanon. Why in the world would Jesus take the disciples to the borderlands? It seems that it's a region where people are open to the Spirit's leading, as Mark 3:8 and Luke 6:17 suggest.[22] Sure enough, a Canaanite woman from that region approaches, shouting at Jesus to heal her daughter. Jesus says nothing (15:23). The disciples respond by telling Jesus to "send her away" (15:23), presumably because she's not one of them, not among God's people but a foreigner and a woman. She's *that*.

We're perplexed when Jesus replies to her cries by saying it's "not fair to take the children's food and throw it to the dogs" (15:26). Did Jesus really call this woman a dog? Is he really showing us there are outsiders who are unworthy of God, unworthy of love, unworthy of healing and wholeness? Or is this a test of what the disciples have learned previously about looking at the heart and not the cultural categories? Jesus calls the religious authorities "blind" and leaves them to stumble about but now proclaims that this woman has "great faith" and heals her (15:28). She can see what is true. Jesus offers a lesson in building bridges, in seeing that we are all children of God. It's a lesson about the heart and about loving God and neighbor enough to travel beyond our cultural constraints to love those who are different. But the disciples haven't yet learned the lesson. Have we? Are we leaders who are stumbling about, unable to see? Or leaders who have taken on the mind of Christ?

There is yet one more aspect of culture we need to touch on briefly before setting aside our understanding of bridge-building as one of the skills enabling us to lead with love: generational differences. Yes, different generations can be considered through the lens of cultures with norms, values, even their own languages. The era in which we are born and the broad context in which we grow up can shape the categories through which we experience the world. We even create categories that help us explain those differences among Boomers, Millennials, Gen Xers, and so on. Generations are formed differently, but it doesn't mean one is "right" and the other "wrong." We need to appreciate, not decry, those differences.

Kinnaman and Matlock, for example, discuss the trend in which "nearly two-thirds of all young adults who were once regular churchgoers have dropped out at one time or another (64 percent)."[23] Younger people are growing up in "an accelerated, complex culture" driven by digital technology, and it shapes their views and engagement of the world.[24] Young adults view authority and institutions with suspicion; not so much for older generations. While going deep into generational cultural characteristics is well beyond the scope of this book, it's important for us to recognize that if we want to lead with love, we also have to care for these generational differences. To impose "our way" as the Boomer generation on Gen Y or Z simply isn't the way of love. We need to build those bridges too. When we begin to accept generational variation as cultural difference, it offers us a way to judge less and learn more about the older or younger group. We can be open to hearing and understanding their experiences in and of the world today. We become relational and offer healing and wholeness to one another.

As our faith develops through spiritual practices of deep listening, as we take on the mind of Christ and our intercultural awareness expands, those scriptural witnesses to the way of Jesus help to break down the categories that value one culture over another. No human culture ever perfectly embodies the way of Jesus. Yet, two thousand years later, followers of Jesus continue to separate and divide according to human cultural categories rather than connecting and bringing to light the relational reality that God has created. We are commanded to embrace our Samaritans, eat meat with pagans, and stop killing others—whether in body or spirit—in the name of Jesus. Jesus shows us that what matters is the heart and our love. Leadership in the name of Christ builds bridges and brings people together in all their beautiful and difficult differences. Why not travel to Tyre and Sidon this week and encounter someone who might just open our eyes to love with the heart of Jesus? We love our neighbor when we can see through their eyes. Learn to see through your neighbor's eyes.

Practice Makes (More but Not Completely) Perfect

1. Take the intercultural development inventory or another cultural-awareness survey and perhaps ask your leadership team or staff to also take the assessment. Most people discover that they are less culturally aware than they believe themselves to be. Reflect on how your stage of intercultural development might impact the way you lead and love others.
2. Work with a mentor or coach who is interculturally competent and whose cultural formation is different from yours. Read books or watch movies that come from cultural perspectives other than your own. Learn a language (try the Duolingo app). Find ways to have new experiences with diverse cultures.

3. Connect with another community of faith that is culturally different from your own. Plan sustained interactions such as joint Bible studies, mission opportunities, and worshipping together periodically. Form relationships that enable both communities to go deeper in hearing and learning about one another's experiences and cultures.

4. Learn about the characteristics of generations other than your own. Invite a group of young adults or teenagers to be in conversation with members of your faith community. Ask them questions and listen carefully. Don't judge or try to "correct" their views.

Resources for Going Deeper

Eberhardt, Jennifer L. *Biased: Uncovering the Hidden Prejudice That Shapes What We See, Think, and Do*. New York: Viking, 2019.

Kang, Jerry. "Immaculate Perception." TedxSanDiego (2013). View this Ted Talk at https://www.youtube.com/watch?v=9VGbwNI6Ssk.

Kinnaman, David, and Mark Matlock. *Faith for Exiles: Five Ways for a New Generation to Follow Jesus in Digital Babylon*. Grand Rapids, MI: Baker Books, 2019.

Nordell, Jessica. *The End of Bias: A Beginning* (New York: Metropolitan Books, 2021).

Visit the Intercultural Development Inventory website at https://idiinventory.com/ and learn more about the intercultural continuum.

❦ 5 ❦

EMBODYING

Leadership Principle Six: Let the Word become flesh in your context

I HAD BEEN at the Village for two years, focused on building relationships, getting to know the people and the surrounding community, hearing their stories and hopes for the future. There had once been glory days, but those were gone. While some longed to return to the past, most realized we needed to move forward as we discovered where Jesus might be leading us. So we formed a strategic planning committee with sixty-year members and ones who had been there for a year. We drew from different generations and ensured that a diverse and representative committee would listen to the Spirit's leading. We examined everything, beginning with what we most valued as a faith community and how we understood our mission. Over several months, a vision was laid out for change and experimentation. We would launch the new strategic plan in January 2020.

Did you just laugh and shake your head? Of course, the plan didn't launch. Instead, we scrambled to adapt to a pandemic that completely shattered expectations and norms for how we do church. And by the time the pandemic was less disruptive and we were again gathering together in the building, the strategic plan no longer fit who we had become over those two years. Now we had Bible studies on Zoom, and participants didn't want to go back to the building for those classes. Not just because of the convenience but also because during the pandemic, we'd invited people to join who lived outside of driving distance. Our livestream of the service had improved greatly, and there were people who wouldn't or couldn't come back to the sanctuary. Livestreaming the service is now a permanent feature of our worship experience. We had created a new way of being community that we embraced. The context changed. We had to adapt. The Word became flesh among us once again, and there was no going backward. Sound familiar?

Leadership in faith communities, if spiritually grounded, will always embody the flesh-and-blood realities of a given place and time. Let the Word become flesh in your context. That's our sixth leadership principle.

Too often, church people resist change. Sometimes we cling to a mythical past that wasn't really as great as our memory wants us to believe. Do we really want to return to a time when segregation existed? A time when women couldn't be in leadership positions or even outside the home? A time when we had telephones with long cords that got tangled? A time before television and radio? A time without aspirin or antibiotics? A time when there wasn't indoor plumbing? The "problem" is that the world and the context keep changing, whether we like it or not. And God calls us to embody the way of Jesus here and now. The past, as the poet Carl Sandburg wrote, "is a bucket of ashes."[1] The past is gone, but it contains the sparks that can ignite something new burning within us and shining brightly in the world.

But change is hard. What are we called to do? Where are we called to serve? How do we reach younger people or "spiritual but not religious" people who are searching for meaning but don't find it in the church? How do we help our people see in new ways? Often, we feel the weight of the problems or challenges we face as leaders of faith communities, but the path doesn't seem clear, or it's blocked by people who are angry or fearful or wistful. *Our* people. The ones we love and want to serve well. Before God's people can change others and help them to travel the way of love, we often have to change ourselves. We need to be open to new ways of existing in the world. We have to allow the Word to become flesh again in us and through us.

Sometimes we think the answer to the problems or issues we face in leadership today—and there have been and always will be problems, challenges, and the need to readjust—can be found and implemented if we have enough money. We hire a consultant. We go to a leadership conference and take home a program that worked in another church. We buy books with how-to tips. But nothing changes. My Villagers tell the story of having hired a consultant some fifteen or twenty years ago. Following a lengthy process and multipage report, the only thing that changed was better signage for the restrooms and fellowship hall.

Unless we learn to read our context in its complexity and ambiguity and develop adaptive capacity in the church by motivating and growing the people, our leadership will flounder. We must take the risk of faith and leave certainty aside. Leading with love requires us to seek change and to pursue justice wherever we might be planted, even when the destination isn't clear. Our sixth leadership principle, then, embodies the gospel as an incarnate reality. The God story always begins with the Word taking on specific, tangible flesh. We are called to lead in particular times, places, and circumstances. We cannot love as God does unless we love the gathered bodies, the human systems that bring us together—and often tear us apart. We lead with love to bring them closer to expressing Jesus's way in the world.

Let's begin by realizing that one context matters above all. That context is the universe that God created and sustains. It is a context revealed to us as the way we are to live in deeply relational, life-giving, and mutually upbuilding communities. Call it the reign of God on earth, the *basileia* that has drawn near in Jesus. Call it the anticipated fullness of the New Creation. This is the context every faith community is called to inhabit and embody in the world. It is a place exemplified by Jesus, who incarnates the Word in the world and reveals to us the way God would have us live: being spiritually attuned, being compassionate toward others, building relationships, furthering life, seeking the justice that enables each person and the created world to thrive, and overflowing with love.

Our leadership is always aiming God's people in the direction of the reign of God as the ideal context to live within. We lead toward the future that God promises and offers us now. But we can't begin to align more closely with this God-given context unless we become careful readers of the contexts, or perhaps subcontexts, in which we live and move and have our being in the world. These are the constraints, opportunities, and conditions we can't ignore as leaders. These contexts are the human constructions of life together that are necessary and helpful but also can and do cause harm. Analyzing our human systems helps us to see where we fall short of God's context and where we need to go in the next faithful step on the way to inhabiting love.

Contemplating Context

There was a time not so long ago when we considered theology to be without context. Many people assumed we understand and share God's Word in a way that is universal or applicable to all. Somehow, we thought we could grasp the gospel apart from it becoming flesh. But over the past fifty or sixty years, it's become clear that we all speak from a location, a perspective shaped by our own cultural formation. Every human being and culture incarnates the Word. For centuries, only those who held power in the United States, almost exclusively white, educated men, could write and speak or lead in society and the church. But the history of liberation and freedom, which biblically begins with God liberating the people from captivity in Egypt, is a history in which dehumanizing systems become named and visible as sinful human constructions that miss the mark of Jesus's way. We have new eyes to see that people don't experience the world and our lives in God like a one-size-fits-all garment.

It shouldn't be surprising that science was making this claim about how particularity shapes our perspective around the same time in the modern era. Einstein's theory of relativity demonstrated that where we are in space and time, our frame of reference, does affect how we perceive an event. His scientific discovery began to unravel the modern idea of a universal perspective. In other words, our location in time and space—and here we might add the human constructs of culture—shapes our understanding of life on earth. We don't live in universals. We live in specifics, in particular historical moments and locations. We embody the Word in concrete expressions. Incarnation is always our calling and our challenge. And if we don't begin with and carry forward the message of the incarnation, we'll never get to the resurrected life God offers. We must discern the contexts in which we are placed if we intend to exercise the faith and hope, the attentive spirit, that lead toward the ideal context of God's way on earth amid our very real differences. We are called to express unconditional and infinite love in specific times, places, and conditions.

So the reign of God that draws near in Jesus is our prototype, our norm for incarnating the gospel. Yet our mission is undertaken not in the abstract but in the very real circumstances of life on earth, where we live. We can act in ways that bring life and flourishing to God's creation, or we can do harm to ourselves, others, and the earth itself. We can't make atoms, molecules, ice caps, mountains, coral reefs, or clouds. Creation is the stuff of life that is given to us. And within these structures of creation, our leadership takes shape within three different contexts or subcontexts, three layers of incarnate life that form the vision and calling for our leadership. If we listen deeply and pay attention, our leadership becomes attuned to the suffering of the world and God's calling to the body of Christ we lead.

We previously mentioned the three primary contexts for leadership in chapter 3, but here we want to explore them in some depth. You might even take a piece of paper and put three headings on it: (1) internal context, (2) external immediate context, and (3) external broad context. Then as we explore what each of these contexts entails, you can begin to list those factors, constraints, and opportunities that exist in your faith community or ministry setting. No two faith communities are alike if we are paying attention and listening to our contexts. Of course, there will be points of overlap among the three contexts, so your columns might have points of overlap. Such analysis is imperfect but can help us to see our situation and mission more clearly. Together, they help us map where and how God might be asking us to change so our faith communities draw nearer to the path we should be walking for the sake of Christ's healing and wholeness in the world.

We might think of context in terms of four concentric circles: the innermost ring is the norm or reign of God as revealed in Jesus. It's the center that holds us together and on which we build or to which we return. The next three circles are the contexts we engage. The second ring represents the internal context. The third ring considers the immediate context of our neighborhood, and the outer ring reflects the broad and, at times, global context that can affect our specific embodiment of the gospel in various ways.

Internal Context
We turn first to what we might call our *internal* context. Here we consider the faith community as it currently exists: things like finances, facilities, the demographics of our people, and the values we hold for life together as an expression of the body of Christ in the world. If you're planting a church, the context might be the school or community center where you gather on Sundays. If your building was erected in the nineteenth century, then you have a very different set of internal circumstances to consider. We're interested in a "balcony" view of our local faith community as it really exists. For example, I once met with a church whose staff said they were a "family." But

their behaviors and actions revealed an insider/outsider dynamic. It wasn't a happy family, if it was a family at all. As a leader, we need to be as objective as possible about the characteristics of our community; all the better if we have trusted members of the faith community who will observe things carefully and add to our analysis. The greater our clarity on the internal context, the better able we are to discern where Jesus might be leading us.

When I was asked to serve as the part-time pastor of Nueva Vida, a bilingual congregation of first- and second-generation persons of Mexican descent, they were worshipping in a tiny, ramshackle house adjacent to the newly constructed but largely unfinished church building. Previous pastors who had demanded changes in the architectural plans created a situation where the building funds ran out. The shell of that church building had existed for several years, but it was uninhabitable. Documentation on required city inspections had been lost. We were repaying the building loan month by month. There were no membership records to be found anywhere, and attendance had dwindled to five or six people. And the church treasurer had disappeared with the checkbook.

To make the context more complicated, providing leadership as a white woman with only a basic command of Spanish required that I learn from God's people about a different set of cultural norms and experiences, even things like which of several words they would use to speak of God's ears. I had no real sense of what it's like to migrate to a new country or to face prejudice because of my name or accent. I couldn't simply walk in and be "in charge" as the pastor. Indeed, we should never assume we know the internal context of any congregation or ministry setting. We had to work together and learn from each other, and I would need to use my privilege in the months ahead to make connections that could help us wrestle with the challenges. We grew together in faith, hope, and love and began to address the challenges one by one.

Perhaps you've been at your church for many years. You might think you understand the internal context inside and out, and you might. But something tends to happen the longer we're in a ministry setting: we no longer see our context well because we are a bit too embedded in it. The narthex might look cluttered or old to visitors, but we just see the narthex. We tend to become accustomed to our context over time. It can be helpful to bring together newer members or to poll visitors about what they see.

We also might conduct a SWOT analysis every few years to analyze the strengths, weaknesses, opportunities, and threats we uncover.[2] I like to revise this analytical framework as SCOPE: strengths, challenges, opportunities, pitfalls, and expectations. What is the SCOPE of your context? Strengths point us to the human and financial resources, the connections and relationships we can draw on. What is our identity and the mission on which we can build? Do we have a powerful worship experience? Do our people love to serve? Maybe we have a lot of great cooks or people who know how to fix things. Maybe we have lawyers or doctors in our faith community. A building without any deferred maintenance can be a strength. Walk through your building, look at your people, and analyze the financial reports. Simply get a clear picture of where the faith community is strong.

Challenges, then, point us to our limitations or constraints, such as a lack of resources. Is the building falling apart or in need of a major renovation? Is our space limited, or do we have too much for our size? What about our financial resources? Are we struggling to pay the bills? Is giving down? Do we have too many people worshipping online and too few in person? Am I, as pastor, expected to do almost everything myself? We can all identify challenges and often more easily than our strengths. But sometimes a challenge is subtler. Perhaps we believe we're great at hospitality, but it's clear visitors don't feel welcome. Or maybe the lay leaders are convinced they're doing new things, but they're really just rearranging the deck chairs. Motivating people and helping them to see things clearly are among the greatest leadership challenges. Here, significantly, we might also need to identify whom we exclude. Who makes us comfortable? Whom do we label as sinners? Who isn't welcome among us? It's impossible to offer love when we're judging and rejecting people. That's a huge challenge. But a challenge is something we can address, even if it's difficult.

Opportunities can begin to connect us beyond the walls in considering our immediate external context. But first, we should consider how to build on our strengths and how we might address our challenges. What do people love about our faith community, and how might we build on those things with our available resources? What's deeply rooted in our identity as a faith community? What do we do well? What resources do we have that are untapped? Do we need to sell off some land or properties? Can we rent out some of our space to nonprofits? What would happen if we changed this or that? Are people joining us online, and can we build relationships with them? Can we begin to stream our service? Do we have skills and gifts among our people that could be employed on behalf of Christ? What might we be able to do? And where do we sense the Spirit at work?

Pitfalls are the obstacles over which we have little control but can make us stumble when pursuing opportunities. Suppose our people are eager to expand our food ministries, but other faith communities nearby are already doing what we're proposing on a large, effective scale. Maybe our denomination has certain requirements for undertaking a ministry that could complicate our efforts. Maybe there are state and federal laws with mountains of paperwork and approvals before we can launch. Maybe we have a faction in the church that will try to undermine our efforts. What if a proposed event or ministry depends on good weather? What if we continue to lose members faster than we are able to reach new people? What are the potential traps we might anticipate and prepare for?

Finally, expectations point us to the emotional and spiritual state of our people. In the context of a faith community, understanding expectations can make all the difference in our ability to lead with love. Here we consider the relational and adaptive capacity that's present. The people's expectations might be a strength, a challenge, or an opportunity, but considering them helps us to map whether the people are open or closed to change, whether they're excited or fearful for the future, whether they trust you or aren't sure about your leadership. Do the people expect the pastor to do everything? To make all the decisions? Do the people expect that the pastor will do exactly what they say? Do the people expect things to be done "the way we've always done them"? Analyzing expectations gives us insight into how willing we are to fall short of them or if we'll feel compelled to cling to the status quo in an effort to preserve our ministry, job, or mental health.

In looking at the SCOPE of our ministry setting, we mostly want to keep our analysis focused on the structures, organization, and resources internal to our faith community before turning our eyes outward from our own system and community. Again, if we think of the ideal community, the reign of God or the *basileia*, as the innermost ring of the concentric circles, then our internal analysis forms the second ring of our context. We ask: How well are we embodying and living out the reign of God that has drawn near in Jesus? What adjustments are necessary for us to more closely align with the way of Jesus? How can we better express the love of God in Jesus Christ and the Holy Spirit right where we live and move and have our being?

External Immediate Context

Once we have considered the SCOPE of the context existing within our community of faith, we can turn to the third level or layer of context: the neighborhood, town, or area in which our ministry exists. Assuming that the mission of God requires us to be the body of Christ in the world and not simply in the building where we gather, worship, and meet, we need to consider how we can best serve the people in our neighborhood. How will we form relationships with them? What needs will we serve? Matthew 25 impels us, for we understand that Jesus is already present and at work in the community:

> "Lord, when was it that we saw you hungry and gave you food, or thirsty and gave you something to eat? And when was it that we saw you a stranger and welcomed you, or naked and gave you clothing? And when was it that we saw you sick or in prison and visited you?" And the king will answer them, "Truly I tell you, just as you did it to one of the least of these who are members of my family, you did it to me." (Matt. 25:37–40)

How interesting that this passage isn't about us "taking Jesus" to others, as if carrying the Ark of the Covenant from the church building, shouting, "We have Jesus!" Rather, we ourselves encounter Jesus whenever we're present to the suffering and needs of others. He's already there, waiting for us to be the body of Christ in our community. We're commanded to engage those who suffer and to provide for the healing and wholeness offered by God. If we are centered in the reign of God as the ideal community, then we are called to love our neighbor as ourselves and to go out to encounter our neighbor with compassion and mercy. Jesus is with them, whether we choose to go beyond our walls or not. This is the reason so many people who participate in missions discover they aren't just helping others but are themselves transformed. Will we listen deeply and discover where Jesus is waiting for us in our local community, even if we're not sure we can do what he asks of us?

We should never forget we're already part of the community, though we can act like an island, surrounded by troubled waters. We may act as if we are keeping Jesus safe inside the building. But the external immediate context is the place where the Word takes on flesh and dwells among us. That Greek word for "dwelt" (*eskenosen*) in John 1:14 translates literally as "pitched a tent" among us. A tent is mobile; the walls are thin places. The Word always travels with the people wherever they go, offers hospitality, and gives life. The Word becomes part of the community. The Word is at work exactly where the tent is pitched.

Sometimes people read the Gospel stories about Jesus's healing miracles through a distorted lens. We see the healing that happened, but we ignore or don't consider the healing that didn't happen. Healing miracles could only take place where the flesh-and-blood Jesus happened to be. There were surely people all over ancient Palestine who needed healing but never encountered Jesus in the flesh or had someone who could run to him on their behalf. That's why Jesus's followers are sent into the world. Not simply to baptize but to bring the world into relationships of healing, wholeness, and abundant life. Salvation is never merely a spiritual confession or an individual condition. It's a lived and embodied reality that reveals that we are inextricably interrelated. It demands that we feed, clothe, visit, extend mercy, and seek justice so that others might experience new and richer life. As the body of Christ, we offer spiritual life (which is far more than a mere confession of Jesus), but we also offer physical life in its fullness in whichever ways we can bring healing and wholeness to people who are vulnerable and suffering. In fact, if we aren't bringing healing and wholeness to others, then we might call ourselves a church, but we really aren't the body of Christ in the world.

There's another aspect of Jesus's healing miracles that we tend to overlook: every person who was healed eventually died. The mystery of this life is that we are to create networks of relationships that offer embodied life here and now, relationships that ease the world's suffering and injustice, while remembering that we're all headed toward the same coda. We're all destined to cross from this life to the next. There is a mystery that envelops the call to heal and upbuild the physical world, which God has created. Nothing lasts forever, we like to say. Yet that which is healed remains present. Matter is never destroyed; it simply rearranges itself. Love never ends. So God declares that all physical matter is good and that we are to care for everything God has created. We should contribute to making the reign of God visible and real here and now. To live and lead with love, we must offer healing and care for those who suffer. To bring moments of healing and deeper connections to those we encounter in our community is the way of love. Salt. Light. Presence.

We can't fix the world; only God can and will in God's timing. But the demand of the gospel commands us to participate in God's healing of the world as the incarnate body of Christ in a particular time and place, called to make a difference among those whom we encounter, knowing we never have the last word and can't bring suffering to an end entirely. Call this mystery the *principle of proximity*. Just as Jesus healed those he encountered face to face, so we are called to do the same. Those who suffer are right outside our doors. The tent flap is open. Our neighbors might even be peeking in. Will we go to them like Abraham running out from the tent to offer hospitality?

Remember the prophet Elijah in 1 Kings 16–17? The text tells us there's a drought engulfing Palestine and the Middle East. Although Elijah is a great man of God, he suffers under the drought and famine, just like everyone else. He's not immune to suffering just because he's a man of faith. And God tells Elijah to go to Zarephath. Imagine Elijah's confusion in being asked to go to a Phoenician city where the gentiles worship Baal. How many "godly" people would resist and refuse to go and live among "those people"? But because Elijah has learned to listen deeply to God and to set aside his own cultural formation and experiences, he goes and encounters the widow with her orphaned son (after all, a woman was property in those days, and the boy was fatherless, so for all practical purposes, he's an orphan).

Elijah lives as a stranger, a foreigner in Zarephath. He "pitches his tent" there, just as God has commanded. He is called by God to become vulnerable. And these three vulnerable people form an unusual community of caring. Alone, they faced death. Together with God and each other, they live. Each has helped just one or two other people, and it makes a difference. We're not called to save the world. Just help the one right before you, and you'll have revealed and added to the relational web that God created in the beginning. We're in this life together, all of us. All people and the whole of God's creation are meant to flourish. We are the body of Christ planted in multiple places in the world to make visible the love, justice, and healing power of Jesus. It's good to help people half a world away who are suffering. But there's someone in need right outside our walls.

It makes a difference, then, whether we are addressing the tangible needs of those who are in proximity to our faith community or are simply doing what we've always done, what we want to do, or what's easiest to accomplish. It's important to know who lives in our community. There are many tools, both free and for purchase, that can assist us in analyzing the surrounding community. Even if we think we know who lives in our small town, we might be surprised by what we find.

The website www.thearda.com is the home of the Association of Religious Data Archives. You can enter your zip code (or adjacent zip codes), click on your church, set a circle of one or two miles around your facility, and pull a report on the demographics of the community. For instance, when I pull a report on my faith community, I find information such as only 39 percent of the population is married, 74 percent is white and 18 percent Black and Latinx, and 88 percent speaks English as their first language. I can begin to think about challenges and possibilities. In this case, maybe we need to focus on supporting unmarried people. Maybe an English as a second language (ESL) class at the church would be an opportunity to serve a need, unless others are already offering ESL classes. If I find many families with young children, a ministry giving diapers or backpacks with school supplies might serve their needs.

But, of course, data is only one piece of the picture. There are other ways to add to our understanding of the external immediate context. One of the most common approaches is to undertake a driving or walking tour of the neighborhood.[3] What are the businesses, if any, that are nearby? Are there daycare centers or assisted living communities? What about grocery stores, restaurants, and food pantries? What kind of housing do we encounter? Do we see many people without homes? To the windshield or walking tour, we can add another source of information: connecting with nonprofits and local government officials in our community. These conversations not only provide us with information about the community but also create potential partnerships for serving the needs of our immediate community. We consider and connect with the relational network that exists in our local community.

Gathering information on the people just beyond our doors helps us to make better decisions about the challenges and opportunities to make a difference. For instance, if we don't understand the language and culture of the people in our neighborhood, we will want to find learning opportunities to know about the culture and norms of those we hope to serve. Or perhaps we'll see an opportunity to be in relationship with those who are unhoused, and we might want to partner with local nonprofits. Again, the external immediate context should be reflected in how we serve and how we ease the suffering and provide healing to those who are vulnerable. Who among us are the widow, the orphan, the stranger, the hungry, the naked, or the person in some form of prison? How will we respond? It's here that we fulfill our mission as the body of Christ. What happens inside the walls of the church should fill us and feed us to send us out to do the work of Christ in a suffering world. The church is a servicing hub, like an airport to the traveler. It's not the destination.

External Broad Context

Finally, the external broad context forms the outer ring of our concentric circles of context. Here we find the contextual factors that will often affect our ministries and require our response, even if they are such broad, even global, realities that we can't hope to "fix" them. We can and often must respond in specific, localized ways. Remember the old saying "Think globally, act locally"? It's a good summary statement for this level of context. All of us who led a faith community through the global pandemic understand this kind of context. When the pandemic began, we had little information with which to make decisions. Most cities and states closed down nonessential businesses, and churches weren't exempt. The context forced us to be and do church differently or to sit back and wait it out. But that choice to do nothing will almost always miss opportunities for Christ to lead us toward something new. Any faith community simply waiting it out meant they weren't interested in building adaptive capacity, which doesn't bode well for the future and its mission on behalf of God.

For most of us, our worship experience had to change. We scrambled to do our services online. Our feeding ministries had to change or temporarily close. Our various gatherings inside the building had to go online or outside. We had to innovate and find new ways of being and doing life together. Some of those adaptations have remained even as the pandemic turned endemic. And, no doubt, many faithful leaders had to confront conflicting views on wearing masks, when and how it was safe to gather, and even if COVID-19 really was an issue. The more we can take on the mind of Christ—spiritually grounded, self-aware, and emotionally intelligent, able to understand different cultural norms and stages of people's faith—the better we are able to love amid such conflict. The scope of the external broad context is simply beyond our full understanding. These broad contextual factors such as the pandemic require a response but are not circumstances we can change. If our church building, the internal context, needs repairs, we can develop a plan to address those things. But in the external broad context, we can only respond in a way that is appropriate to our particular, local incarnate existence. We may join with others to make a difference in the midst of such suffering. But we aren't going to end the broad contextual concern.

At times, the external broad context can feel like a heavy weight laid on us: political turmoil across the nation, racial injustice, changing laws that seem right or wrong, an opioid epidemic, climate change, wars, drought and famine, increasing numbers of "spiritual but not religious people," declining rural populations, migration, and the list goes on. Sometimes the broader context appears overwhelming, even paralyzing. But, again, we can't fix the whole world. That's not our calling in Christ. And it's a spiritual practice to trust that God is at work in a very broken world, a world consumed by suffering, violence, death, and hatred. Our deep listening should enable us to trust that God is walking amid this rubble, and it should help us to hear the response that is ours to make as the body of Christ in a particular time and place. We aren't called to ignore the suffering but to engage it as the body of Christ. To touch real people who are hurting. We heal and bring hope to those in our time and place.

If the country is becoming less "religious," then perhaps our leadership ought to help our people become less concerned about "the church" and its rules, beliefs, and judgment and more focused on the spiritual riches of Christ manifesting as love, justice, and abundant life that weaves together all things in the world. Don't try to fix the whole world. Just do what is possible right where you are. What can our faith community do to address racial injustice in our city or town? How can we assist those who are migrating to our area from Afghanistan, Ethiopia, or Venezuela? If you live in a location that has been affected by climate change resulting in fires, drought, flooding, and so forth, you might need to respond to that context and prepare for future needs that will arise. Perhaps your faith community lives in a city that has significant infrastructure problems, such as a lack of clean water. How will you, as the body of Christ, respond? Again, the principle of proximity leads us to help those we encounter in the places where we exist as flesh and blood. We are a living eucharistic expression, body and blood, given to all.

Understanding the institutional, systemic level is vital. Sometimes it's not about feeding or visiting an individual but confronting human systems that are dehumanizing and death-dealing. Who is better equipped to join in a web or network of relationships than the people of God planted across the world? Our strength as God's people arises from our incarnate existence as the body of Christ in specific locations that should be linked across the world as one body with the mind of Christ. The potential to grow into this one body with its many parts can only be realized as we grow in deep listening, learn to love before we judge or insist on our thought patterns, and accept differences that exist in the ways human beings organize life together. The potential for the one body of Christ to stir up God's reign on earth and alleviate suffering is enormous.

If you've made columns to consider the different contexts, you might want to indicate which, if any, of the broad contextual factors require a response from your faith community and which are important but don't rise to the level of your mission, at least until a disaster or crisis strikes nearby. What broad factors do you find you can't ignore in leading your faith community well? What does love require of your faithful people? Remember, leading with love means always looking to God's future. We are to lead in ways that further the flourishing of life before death is at the doorstep.

The Bigger Picture Helps Us to Love Others

Once we have mapped out the internal context, the external immediate context, and the external broader context that affect our incarnate expression of the body of Christ, we can assess who we are called to be for the sake of Christ in the world. First, though, we need the fourth column, the anchor for our analysis: the context of the reign of God that has drawn near in Jesus Christ. The more we are attuned, attentive, and listening to and for the ideal context or the love of God in Jesus Christ in the Holy Spirit erupting into the world, the more that way of love will become our primary mode of engaging those we live among. The way of love becomes our central identity, even as other realities shape and form us. Don't list what your community believes and its rules. Map out the kind of life that Jesus pours out in love, humility, and compassion. Alleviate suffering. Invite the outsider to eat and walk with you. Break the rules when they harm others. Question institutional practices that cause harm. Feed five thousand. Calm a storm. Love with abandon. When we open ourselves to love, it leads us to become Jesus in the suffering world.

Our analysis can indicate that one of the three contexts might drive our leadership at a particular time and place. If you find yourself in a faith community that has lost half its members over a year or two, and those who remain are angry, depressed, and exhausted, you'll need to focus first on the internal context. Your leadership will be one of loving the people until they are healed and can begin again to pour out God's love into the world beyond the walls. Churches filled with broken or judgmental people will have a hard time loving their neighbor until they've learned to love themselves in all their own imperfections. If your neighborhood is faced with an epidemic of high school students overdosing, you might find that your calling is to love young people in ways that will alleviate grief, provide hope for the future, and encourage an end to the drug crisis. Perhaps your faith community is well equipped to reach those who consider themselves spiritual but aren't connected to community and in life-giving relationships. Maybe your faith community is multiethnic and perfectly positioned to address racism in your neighborhood or city. Your contextual map can offer insights for leading with love.

Where is your faith community falling short, missing the mark, when it comes to the context of the reign of God and our calling in Jesus Christ? Listen to what the Spirit is saying. Don't be afraid to envision the future. If our leadership is only about the survival of the church, we've lost sight of

Jesus and his way. After all, if you have a vision statement, its very purpose is to serve as a guide for where you are to go on behalf of God's mission in the world, not where you desperately wish to remain. Maybe we all need to rewrite our vision statements to simply say: Love. Love more. Love God and neighbor and ourselves with abandon. Love the earth God has given us. Pack up our tent and get moving. Go and let love shape and reform, healing everything it encounters.

Analyzing and assessing our context should be considered a spiritual practice we undertake to see and hear where God is leading us. We want to take on the mind of Christ. We want to listen deeply to God. We want to see who we are, who we are to serve, and how we can best mobilize our resources to bring life in abundance to others. Whether we are feeding a dozen people or five thousand doesn't matter. Do what is within your means to do.

Seeing and hearing require us to act. And we all know that even if the leaders are willing, often the people are reluctant. They fear change. Or they're afraid things they care about deeply will be lost in the process of change. But every living thing changes, even if we try to cling to the past or the status quo. Unless we learn to love in deeper and new ways, we'll miss our calling in Christ. How, then, do we lead with the kind of love that changes both the people of God and the people we are called to serve so that love might flourish? Let's turn to the important work on adaptive change and adaptive leadership, which provides tools for today's complex context.

Embodying Adaptive Capacity

If we keep God at the center of our mission and vision, adaptive leadership is among the most helpful approaches for leading with love. After all, without the deep listening we've suggested throughout this book, we can have a human organization, even one that's doing well, but we aren't developing disciples, learners, and followers of Jesus Christ. They won't be taking on the mind of Christ, and we won't be helping people live in the reign of God that has drawn near. But with God at the center of the practice, important pieces come together.

The theory of adaptive change comes from the work of Ronald Heifetz, Martin Linsky, and Alexander Grashow of Harvard University and, in the context of Christian faith, has been explored by Tod Bolsinger and Kevin Ford of Leighton Ford Ministries, among others. You might be familiar with the practice of adaptive leadership, and here we simply want to provide a brief overview of the key dimensions of this leadership practice, especially as it relates to growing in love and enabling the Word to become flesh in our place and time. How do adaptive processes enable us to lead with love?

By definition, adaptive change is "the process of mobilizing people to tackle tough challenges and thrive."[4] Heifetz et al. explain that "the concept of thriving is drawn from evolutionary biology, in which a successful adaptation has three characteristics: (1) it preserves the DNA essential for the species' continued survival; (2) it discards . . . the DNA that no longer serves the species' current needs; and (3) it creates DNA arrangements that give the species the ability to flourish in new ways and in more challenging environments."[5] Remember that scientific truth should inform our lives on earth. Adaptation is about promoting abundant life. Science is given by God to help us better understand the processes and structures of creation.

Suppose instead of speaking about the "species" in the above quote, we use "the gospel" as the primary reality that shapes the body of Christ. In other words, we preserve the gospel as essential, we discard expressions of the gospel that no longer meet our needs, and we rearrange our expression of the gospel to flourish in new ways and new contexts. Biological organisms adapt over time to the context and to what produces health and life. Collectively, human beings also adapt and find ways to improve life, though those improvements often come with unanticipated new problems to solve. If we think of the faith community as the body of Christ, then biological processes can help to illuminate who we are and how we must recreate our lived expression of the incarnate Word across time and space. Every living thing changes pretty much constantly, even if at the cellular level. Think of it this way: we have to "fit" the realities within which we are planted if we hope to share the good news, bring hope to a suffering world, and enable the reign of God to draw near.

This isn't a call to jettison the gospel in favor of whatever works. Quite the opposite. The gospel is the one essential piece of our DNA. Sometimes, however, we equate our expression of the gospel with the gospel itself. When we recognize with the mind of Christ that the gospel takes on flesh in each generation through us and our faithfulness to Christ, it enables us to hold on to the faith, hope, and love poured out in Jesus and re-form our human embodiment of the gospel in a particular time and place. The first Christians met in houses and had no books of liturgy, bulletins, or musical instruments. The church in the nineteenth century thought cathedrals, Sunday schools, fancy clothes, and pipe organs were essential. Today, we often have praise bands, small discipleship groups at various times, pastors in skinny jeans, and electronic giving.

We must adapt to our contexts if we seek to be healthy and thrive. Adapting to the context doesn't mean we emulate the surrounding culture. Indeed, if we've formed a healthy and vibrant Christ culture among our people, it will be their guiding way of life. Like a physical body, there are signs or indicators of health or illness in the body of Christ. A doctor checks vital signs to assess the state of the body. Leaders of faith communities need to assess a different set of vitals. These vitals alongside our contextual analysis can enable us to discern where we need to change and adapt.

Taking Your Faith Community's Vitals

One helpful set of indicators comes from the Transforming Church Insight (TCI) survey conducted by Kevin Ford since 1999, which draws on thousands of churches across denominations and nondenominational associations. Since publishing his 2008 book, *Transforming Church*, Ford has closed his consulting firm and now operates his survey and analysis of healthy churches from within Leighton Ford Ministries. The survey addresses five areas of church health or vitality: community, code, calling, cause, and change.[6]

Community, the first indicator, refers to internal relationships that provide the sense of a loving, caring, warm, close-knit community. It's about a sense of belonging. We might ask: Do the people in our faith community feel their needs and faith development are well supported? Are they known and cared for? Community is about whether relationships flourish within the faith community.

Code points to the vision, purpose, and goals of the congregation and how well these are communicated to and embraced by the people. Key questions related to a church's code might include: Why do we exist? Where are we being led? Whom are we called to serve? Code also includes worship, opportunities to learn and grow, and the building itself (which, interestingly, isn't a good indicator of whether or not a church is healthy). These things all shape our identity or, we might even say, our culture. In fact, Ford's research suggests that one of the most important factors in the vitality of a faith community is a clear vision that is well articulated and embraced by the people, not just the leaders. Remember, leadership in faith communities is about enabling God's reign to draw near as we pursue the future that God is calling us to embody. If we don't know where we are headed, we are sure to find ourselves wandering in circles in the wilderness.

Ford's third indicator, calling, includes respect for different points of view and how leadership handles difficult issues and conversations. Calling also includes transparency around finances and wise stewardship of resources. In some ways, data suggest that calling might be the least impactful of the five areas, though still of importance to our mission and vitality. Next, cause refers to the ways we connect with the surrounding community and address its needs and whether that community values our outreach ministries and relationships. The percentage of our people directly involved in the outreach doesn't appear to be a strong indicator of a faith community's health, even as that missional work is an important overall contributing factor. Cause also includes the effectiveness of children, youth, and family ministries, or what we might think of as the learning and growing aspect of our life together. Finally, Ford's TCI survey addresses change, which relates to things like innovation, a sense of cutting-edge ministry, and creativity. Change also includes the implementation of our vision and goals. Healthy faith communities don't just envision the future; they also enact those visions and involve and motivate the people to bring them into existence.

While survey data certainly don't tell us everything, and surveys always involve the perception of insiders, it nonetheless identifies a set of characteristics or areas that might help us take the pulse of our faith community and consider what should be preserved and where we might need to change. Are there areas among the above five that we know need attention? Is there some area that seems to be undermining our mission and requires tweaking or overhauling? Remember that asking the right questions is one of the most important things we can do in our leadership.

The TCI points us toward characteristics of healthy faith communities, but it doesn't tell us how we should bring these elements to life. That's the task of leadership, and it's the piece that requires contextualization. In most cases, we can't just take some other faith community's program or way of doing things and implement it. It has to fit who and where we are. Asking about our community, code, cause, calling, and change provides us with a way of seeing what's happening and where we need to rethink our life together for the sake of Christ in the world. When we begin to see those things that need to change, how do we enact that change? We are called by faith to look forward in faith, hope, and love and to discern where Jesus is leading.

It's possible to turn to the Scriptures for another measure of the health and vitality of a local faith community. When we remember that a faith community is always a human organization created by people to enable the mission and life of the spiritual body of Christ, then we need a measure of that spiritual health. We often measure the human institution via numbers of members, budgets, professions of faith, and so on. But these measures seldom get at the spiritual dimension. How do we know if our faith community is open to God's Spirit or stuck in human patterns? One scriptural measure of spiritual health is offered to us by Paul in his letter to the Galatians. It's what we know as "the fruit of the Spirit" (Gal. 5:22–23).

In the ancient world, this image or metaphor would have been readily understood. They lived in an agricultural society. So many of us today live in urban contexts where fruit comes from a bin in the grocery store that I pay for, and then the fruit is mine. Or I order five apples online, and an unseen hand drops them at my front door. Today, receiving fruit is transactional: I do this; I get that. The one time when Jesus was really angry in the Gospels, turning over the tables in the Temple, he was upset about life in God being reduced to a transaction (Matt. 21:12–13). But Paul's Galatians would have understood that bearing fruit is a process that takes place between God and the fruit-bearer. God provides the tree or vine, the sun, the rain, and the earth. But the orchard owner has to till the soil, pull the weeds, prune the trees, keep birds and bugs away, and harvest at the right time. We sometimes think that if we believe in Jesus, then fruit of the Spirit is magically given to us. That's not what Paul or Jesus would have meant. The farmer can't simply go to the door in the morning and yell, "I believe in you, orchard!" Then go back to bed. It takes spiritual practice to open ourselves to the Spirit so that good fruit might come forth and feed the world with the love of God in Jesus Christ.

Often, we read Paul's discussion of the fruit of the Spirit as qualities of individuals. But in the context of his letter, it's quite likely he's also suggesting that the body of Christ, the community gathered as the *ekklesia*, should reflect the qualities of love, joy, peace, patience, kindness, generosity, faithfulness, and self-control (Gal. 5:22). Paul writes to the Galatians to correct their desire to reestablish the Jewish law as a requirement for life in the church. He goes so far as to say, "You who want to be justified by the law have cut yourselves off from Christ" (Gal. 5:4). The laws, rules, regulations, restrictions—*this*, not *that*—will never bring forth the fruit of the Spirit. Instead, rules and regulations demanding a certain morality first will evoke in the community the "works of the flesh" (Gal. 5:19) or the weeds of the world.

Remember how brain science has helped us see that we have to learn how to love first if we hope for morality to be present? If you teach a child to follow rules and to know right from wrong, which is important for the child's development, but you don't love and nurture that child, they'll likely grow up to be a bitter, finger-pointing person. But if they know they're deeply loved and cared for, they will want to do what is right and good. And so it goes with the faith community as well. If we begin with rules and the law, we'll end up exhibiting the qualities of the flesh or the world, whether embracing immorality or rejecting the love and reconciliation poured out by the Spirit. So alongside "fornication, impurity, licentiousness . . . drunkenness, carousing" are characteristics that destroy love: "enmities, strife, jealousy, anger, quarrels, dissensions, factions, envy" (Gal. 5:19–20). If a church is filled with factions, anger, arguments, and judgment, it cannot and will not be of the Spirit. Those weeds of the world will first need to be pulled if the good fruit is to come forth.

Paul's letter to the Galatians is clear. If we aren't putting love first, we'll find ourselves looking just like the world, which always argues about who's right, better, holier, stronger, and so on. And there it is: the sin of comparisons. It's not the one who loves deeply who ignores morality; it's the one who tries to be godly by means of rules, laws, and judgment. Even the Ten Commandments are, at heart, the moral code that suggests how best to love God and love others. It's the particular circumstances of life from which the law arises: I know it says, "Do not kill," but what if I'm a soldier defending our people? Is it okay then? I know it says, "Honor your father and mother," but what if my dad beat me and my mom all the time? How do I "honor" his violence? The law arises from the Ten Commandments, which provide guidelines for how to love. But Jesus has fulfilled the law. He commands but one law.

Paul is clear that "the only thing that counts is faith working through love" (Gal. 5:6). He's clear that freedom from the law in Jesus Christ isn't "an opportunity for self-indulgence, but through love become slaves to one another" (Gal. 5:13). "For the whole law," says Paul, "is summed up in a single commandment, 'You shall love your neighbor as yourself'" (Gal. 5:14). Love is everything, says Paul. If you aren't learning to love, you'll not find joy, peace, patience, kindness, generosity, faithfulness, and self-control present in the body of Christ. You'll find arguments, criticism, and factions, and those things will lead to immorality. Without love, we'll never arrive at the moral life. Ask yourself, as a leader: What qualities does my faith community tend to exhibit? Do I lead in a way that causes divisions and arguments? Or is love the main thing among us? Measure the spiritual health of the body of Christ.

The Process of Adaptive Leadership

As we return to the practice of adaptive leadership, there are a few key elements of the process we want to consider. We begin by recognizing that adaptive change takes time. Leading a faith community in a different direction is more like steering an ocean liner than a speed boat: we can't turn quickly but must be prepared to stay steady on the wheel to go in a new direction. We live in a consumeristic culture where we expect immediacy, getting what we want right now delivered to our doorstep with a click of our mouse. But adaptation doesn't happen in a moment; it can't be downloaded or delivered in a day. Sometimes people think a good leader is decisive and acts swiftly. In adaptive change, that's not really a healthy approach.

For the most part, Jesus didn't lead in a way that moved quickly. He simply circled around his message over and again, acted in consistent ways, and invited people to get on board and to follow where he was leading. Some did. Some walked away. Remember, 1 Corinthians 13:4 tells us that love is patient. We might even suggest that we await the *kairos* moment, God's time, by faithfully and hopefully walking the path laid out before us. If we give up too quickly, the Spirit's work will be cut short. If we move too fast, we'll not see where the Spirit is leading. Embodying the gospel anew for the sake of Christ in the world takes patience. Good adaptive leadership is about slow and steady steps, small steps, in the direction we need to go.

But those small steps often are painful. In fact, one of the key aspects of adaptive leadership is to intentionally disrupt the status quo and the comfort level of the people. Then we'll have to manage their disappointment with our leadership. To move adaptively, we find ourselves in the difficult position of challenging some of the people's expectations. Stop for moment and think about the things your people might expect—or that the more vocal among them might tell you. I once heard about a church that insisted on using a hymnal from 1935 and refused any "newer" music. Another church insisted the only Bible they would use was the paraphrased Good News version, and yet another that upheld the King James version as the "real" Bible. Do the people expect the pastor to make all the decisions? Are there certain lay members who always get the final word on any matter? Is there a yearly event that no longer serves the purpose for which it was created, but people won't let it go? Is our mission outreach no longer serving the community, but it's what we've always done? Challenging expectations is often hard work. We need to move slowly, care for the people's feelings and contributions, and recognize how far we can go at a given time. Sometimes, we might need to back up a little when we sense we've pushed too far. Our job is to "raise the temperature" and be prepared to address pushback as we "anticipate and counteract tactics that people will use to lower the heat to more comfortable levels."[7]

Ronald Heifetz and Martin Linsky associate good leadership with this idea of controlling the temperature. Whenever we seek to change the status quo—something that is generally quite resistant to change in faith communities—"hidden conflicts" will bubble to the surface.[8] And most pastors don't like conflict. Thus, our grounding through deep listening and emotional intelligence is essential to this work of adaptive leadership since leaders "can't expect the group to tolerate more stress than you can stand yourself."[9] As the authors explain, we raise the temperature or challenge the status quo enough that people feel the heat. The old adage of comforting those afflicted and afflicting those who are comfortable comes to mind. Adaptive leadership is about stirring things up enough that people aren't simply going through the motions. But the second aspect of controlling the temperature is knowing when to back off and lower the stress level. Reducing the heat isn't about accepting the status quo or giving up on the challenges. It's about finding ways to remind the people they are loved, there are things they do well as the body of Christ, and the things that matter most to them—the essential DNA—will remain. Did Jesus understand how to regulate the temperature? After all, asking questions and stopping to feed a lot of people seem to be strategies for lowering the temperature and taking a break from challenging the status quo.

As we lead adaptive change, we'll also need to understand and explain the difference between technical problems and adaptive challenges. A technical problem has available answers. Sometimes, faithful people will reach for the low-hanging fruit. We'll solve a technical problem and feel good about what we've done. But it can be a red herring, a distraction through which we avoid acknowledging the hard work we need to do. Sometimes faith communities pursue technical answers in addressing complex adaptive challenges. While technical fixes can help, they'll seldom take us very far and may serve to gloss over the hard work that must be done. When the pandemic hit, it was a technical challenge for many of us to stream our worship services online. We might have needed some expertise and money, but the answers were widely available. Yet, as some pastors discovered, not every faith community was willing to go online. That's a different question and probably rooted in an adaptive challenge: "Adaptive challenges are typically grounded in the complexity of values, beliefs, and loyalties rather than technical complexity and stir up intense emotions."[10]

Here's an example of how technical answers can become a subterfuge. Suppose your attendance is declining, and people say, "We need to get more visitors." So the decision is made to send out a mailer every quarter inviting people to visit Whata Church. The problem, of course, is that mailers don't seem to make a difference in this day and age. It's a technical solution for a much more complex problem that requires an adaptive response. And worse, we never ask the question of whether anyone has come to visit after receiving our mailer. We don't get any feedback. Nothing changes. But we act as if we've taken hold of the problem and solved it. Adaptive challenges simply don't have easy answers or quick fixes. We might have to change in some ways that make us uncomfortable. How often have you found yourself leading exactly this kind of fruitless endeavor? It's a big step forward to acknowledge the adaptive challenge before you rather than to sidestep it because, well, it does seem daunting. A mailer doesn't raise strong feelings. Dealing with the adaptive change just might. But with the spiritual disciplines we've already discussed in previous chapters, it's a bit more manageable. With love, all things are possible. Remember, faith is never about certainty. It's about trusting in God and stepping faithfully and hopefully toward the emerging future.

At its best, adaptive leadership involves a careful, well-considered, measured process. Good process tends to lead to good outcomes. Here we can only provide the most basic overview of the process presented by Heifetz et al. They construct a simple "two-by-two diagnosis matrix" to summarize the process, and I'll add to this matrix in the figure below.[11] You'll see that reflection, getting "on the balcony" to observe the workings of the community (the *system*) and engage in self-reflection as the leader, is a necessary step to move to the actions of mobilizing the people and managing yourself throughout the process. When it's time to act, we acknowledge that because adaptive challenges don't have easy answers, the only way to begin addressing the issue is to experiment. Try things that are new and different or might help to deal with the challenge. Sometimes we can even use the language of experimentation to keep the "heat" at an acceptable level. And then we monitor whether the experiment makes a difference or not (fig. 5.1).

After I had served the Village for a year or two, it was clear that in our rebuilding process, we couldn't sustain two worship services. Prior to my arrival, the congregation had decided to have a traditional service at 9:00 a.m. and a contemporary one at 11:00 a.m., with Sunday school in between. But the numbers in attendance at both services were small, the sanctuary looked empty, and visitors felt underwhelmed. We needed to combine them into a blended service, but the prospect satisfied no one. Most people preferred a certain style of worship. They preferred a particular time to attend.

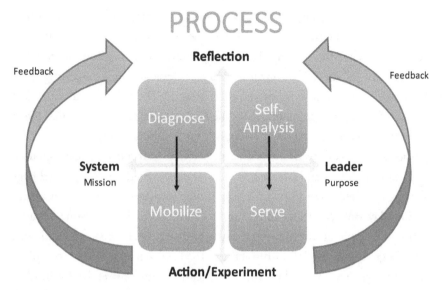

Figure 5.1: Adaptive Process
Adapted from Ronald Heifetz, Alexander Grashow, and Marty Linsky, *The Practice of Adaptive Leadership: Tools and Tactics for Changing Your Organization and the World* (Boston: Harvard Business Press, 2009), 6.

There was no easy answer. Some people pushed to combine the services, while others were unwilling to change their expectations. I waited and observed and listened. I tried to get onto the "balcony." Admittedly, I didn't really have a good idea of how to address this dilemma. But I paid attention and reflected on the situation a lot.

As summer approached, I saw an opening and announced that we would combine the two services only in the month of July as an experiment. After all, with so many people traveling in the summer, it just made sense to have one service, at least in July. The language of experimentation lowered the temperature. And something pretty amazing happened. The people decided they preferred being together, even if it meant some of the music and maybe the worship time weren't their preference. It meant Sunday School classes would have to decide either to meet at nine or at eleven. I did hear from people who were unhappy with one thing or another, but the value of seeing each other gathered as one body ultimately prevailed. People adjusted. And we never went back after that July experiment.

I don't want to suggest that all experiments are successful. I don't want to suggest that most of my experiments have been successful. In fact, many don't work very well. After hearing about a diaper ministry being done at churches in Kansas, I suggested that our missions team look at doing something similar to reach the young families in our community. We only have a handful of young adults and young families in our faith community, so it seemed like a good way to connect and build relationships. Reaching young adults with the gospel is a tremendous adaptive challenge today. Our missions team set up a registration online, and over a hundred families signed up. We packed bags for one hundred according to the size of diapers they needed. But on diaper pickup day, only twenty or thirty families showed up. The experiment wasn't a failure, but something about it didn't work well. We weren't sure it allowed us to begin building relationships either. The feedback loop told us to explore different avenues, to build on what we'd learned. You've been in this kind of situation. The question is: Did you try to do the same thing again? I don't need to remind you that's the definition of insanity: doing the same thing and expecting different results. Or did you experiment with a different way to reach people? It might take many experiments, but as scientists know, each supposed "failure" eliminates one potential solution and leads us closer to an answer. "Try and try again" is the motto for adaptive leadership.

While there is much more to the process than this very simplified overview, it gives us a basic sense of how adaptation works. Remember, leadership in faith communities is about faithful and hopeful attention to grow into God's promised future of love and justice such that it draws near in a particular time and place. And above all, our leadership is about the people. God's people. It's about motivating, encouraging, and, most of all, loving the people toward change that better expresses and enacts God's mission in the world.

Most of us really do desire to love and serve God and others. What looks like fear of change may really be fear of loss.[12] Some people complain when we remove the old candlestick holders from the altar. It's not that they love those tarnished brass monstrosities. What they love is the memories of people and times that meant a great deal to them. Maybe their grandmother donated them. Maybe when they were married in the sanctuary, they looked right at those candlestick holders. We equate certain objects or practices with past people and events that matter to our sense of loving and being loved.

We can't lead as if we don't care about those connections. Instead, we must lead in a way that makes God's people feel loved, valued, and cared for even as they might grieve a cherished past.

Our leadership is unique in the sense that—except for perhaps a few staff members—all our people are volunteers. All of them choose to seek God and serve Jesus Christ in and through our particular faith community. It is and should be a place of relational well-being for them. We want to feel safe and valued in the faith community. Our emotions and the things we care about matter greatly. Again, the most important skill for leading with love will always be the quality of the relationships we develop through our listening and presence, through knowing the name of every member of our congregation or of our area of ministry, by recognizing that each person has an unseen web of relationships and experiences, deep down in their brain below the cortex, that will always remain part of their life in the community. If people don't sense that you love them, they won't trust your leadership. At this point, we can see the value of our spiritual grounding in deep listening and emotional intelligence, in understanding cultural realities and contextual matters. The people need to know we love God and we love them with all their experiences, wounds, and memories.

Adaptive leadership is a key skill for being the body of Christ and bearing good fruit in our rapidly changing world. Our contextual analysis inevitably points us toward community or societal issues beyond our walls that need to change as well. Adaptive principles and the adaptive process that examines the system and the self before moving into action can also apply to our engagement of justice and caring for the widow, the orphan, and the stranger. The individual in the process outlined above, the "leader" in our diagram, now must be thought of as the faith community itself and how it can respond to make a difference in changing systems beyond the walls of our faith community. If we wish to love as Jesus loved, then we must express a concern for healing and justice in the world.

Embodying Justice

Turning to justice late in this conversation about leadership might strike some as an afterthought. You might want to push back and suggest that justice ought to be the first word. Or perhaps you think leading a faith community isn't about justice at all. But without justice, which is a central concern throughout the scriptural witnesses, love will be lacking. To love, writes Thomas Jay Oord, "is to act intentionally, in relational response to God and others, to promote overall well-being."[13] But for Oord, "overall" points toward justice: "Lovers consider how localized actions affect wider well-being."[14] He goes on to say that justice refers to "acting for the good of all in a restorative sense, especially the neglected or mistreated."[15] We are called by God to think about social capital, fairness, and the well-being of the whole of creation.

Leading with love requires a deep concern for the widow, the orphan, the stranger, those who are poor, and any among us who are vulnerable, excluded, unable to access the resources and life others take for granted. These are people who often end up in a place of vulnerability because of human systems and institutions. These are the very people to whom Jesus goes. And his care for those who are vulnerable often leads him to be criticized by the religious authorities or the system makers and keepers. It's an age-old story that plays out in the prophets of the Hebrew Scriptures. Their job isn't to predict the future. It's not to point out the people's personal sins. Their job isn't even to announce judgment. The prophet speaks God's Word to those in the community to reveal their failures to love and care for those who are vulnerable as God does. The prophet seeks to address systemic, institutional harm.

Understanding the role of the prophet is important if we hope to address injustice in our world. Biblical scholar Ellen Davis identifies a number of key elements of the prophetic role. First, what I have called the *principle of incarnation* is reflected in the prophetic perspective: "The radical concreteness of prophetic expression, which both engages the hearers in particular contexts and makes vivid God's engagement with the world."[16] Prophets speak to a particular time, place, and context to bring love to light. Second, prophets are concerned with the kind of justice that exists not as a personal or individual commitment but as a communal reality as the "moral, economic, and religious integrity in human communities . . . and the recognition that human integrity in these several dimensions is fundamentally related to the God-given integrity of creation."[17] Human systems require accountability whenever they undermine love.

Third, Davis points us toward God's expectation that the prophet will be in solidarity with those who suffer within our societies and world.[18] Love goes out to the places where people need healing and wholeness. These three concerns, which relate to justice in a communal sense, are tied by Davis to two additional prophetic elements:

> 4. *The prophet as the trusted friend of God, entrusted with a ministry of protest, prayer, healing, and reconciliation*
> 5. *Prophetic witness to the theological significance of those who do not worship Israel's God, which is potentially a witness of reconciliation.*[19]

The prophet speaks to the community and human organizations, seeking to share in God's suffering with those who are vulnerable and excluded and to announce healing, liberation, systemic change, and reconciliation with God and all of God's creation. The prophet, including Jesus in his prophetic role, seeks justice, fairness, equity. Leading with love requires us to do the same.

To arrive at a place where justice is embodied in our leadership and faith community as an aspect of the way of love, we need those things we've discussed to this point: deep listening, learning and growing, pursuing emotional intelligence, addressing bias in ourselves and our people, and developing intercultural awareness and capacity. These spiritual practices ground the quality and depth of our love and action in the world. Our pursuit of justice, as God's justice, requires that we take on the mind of Christ so that we might love as God loves. We all know that sometimes the pursuit of justice becomes an end in itself rather than being integrally linked to leading with love. Sometimes we take up our bullhorn and march, then march again, and post our marching and message on social media. But that won't change people or the situation. There must be more to our pursuit of justice. Justice is to give life, to create relationships, and to build up. Justice reveals the living God. Justice brings love to light and to fruition. Justice reconciles and makes whole. So how do we tear down that which obstructs justice so that all are held within the way of love?

To begin, we turn to the Hebrew Scriptures and the New Testament, where justice is a central concern. Our biblical translations can, at times, obscure the cry for justice. In Hebrew, the primary word for "justice" is *mish-pat,* and according to Tim Keller, there are more than two hundred usages of the word in the Old Testament (using the New International Version).[20] It is also translated into English as "righteousness," which gives people the opportunity to turn it into personal morality. Thus, we hold fast to our false sense of moral purity: "But I've never owned slaves." "I don't even know any child laborers in Indonesia." But thus says the Lord: those claims to "personal holiness" aren't how the ancient people would have understood *mishpat.*

As with Indigenous communities today, those people of the twelve tribes of Israel likely thought of themselves, first and foremost, as a *we,* as a community.[21] The idea of an autonomous self and its personal moral center comes later in Western intellectual history. Central to biblical justice is the strength of a community and its relationships. How we live together precedes any notion of my rights or righteousness as an individual. The emphasis is placed not on "my rights" but what we today might call *social capital,* or the notion that we prioritize the greater good, knowing that my own well-being is tied up with the thriving of the whole.[22] I might not benefit directly today through my generosity or service, but someday I will be the one in need, and the community will hold me together. From a gospel lens, that's how communities are intended to function. Acts 2:44–5 and 4:32 aren't about socialism; they point to social capital.

The gospel proclaims radical relationship as the essence of the way of Jesus Christ. Right relationship is at the heart of love and justice. And *mish-pat* points to receiving what is due, making things right, and providing the victim or the one lacking access with fair recompense. Justice requires us to care for the most vulnerable—the widow, the orphan, and the stranger or foreigner—exactly because the community has created structures that prevent some from having fair access to what others take for granted. It's not the categories that matter. They point us toward whomever our society or community marginalizes and excludes. Those who are faced with a scarcity of resources at no fault of their own. Who are the widow, the orphan, and the stranger in your own community?

Ultimately, justice is about what I'm doing to others and whether I might be participating in a system that is good for me but excludes or harms others. It's about life-giving relationships and our recognition that we are all woven together in this universe by the Creator, Redeemer, and Sustainer. God doesn't create systems of exclusion; human beings do. And our human systems tend to set up barriers for some, often based on some physical characteristic (race or ethnicity, gender, sexuality, age, disability, etc.). God's way invites us to be a community in which justice is central to the quality of our love.

The concept of systemic sin is crucial if we wish to understand justice as it relates to leading with love. We are either in this together and at work to create healthy, life-giving relational structures, or we aren't following Jesus. Systemic sin reveals the ways our life together creates scarcity, sets up barriers, and deprives some of life while adding to the privileges and purses of others. If I buy a pair of shoes at a low price but only because the workers in Thailand were paid pennies to cobble that pair, then I'm contributing to systemic sin. I'm depriving some of a fair and just wage because I like to pay less for my shoes. Most of the time, scarcity and barriers are the result of human actions, not simply "the way things are." But "in the face of systemic scarcity, the gospel signifies abundant life, not simply in a spiritual sense, but in the sense of the basic material provisions necessary for a life of flourishing."[23] It requires us to seek change in systems, organizations, and structures—including the church—that create barriers and exclude some in favor of others.

This brings us to a second Hebrew word that speaks to justice, *tzadeqah*, which "refers to day-to-day living in which a person conducts all relationships in family and society with fairness, generosity, and equity."[24] The Hebrew understanding of *tzadeqah* points to a way of living with others that creates a society in which all are cared for. This kind of society, the way of love, begins with our life together in radical relationship. The mind of Christ enables us to see how God's creation is interrelated, even if we choose to close our eyes and hearts. God's people are called to share our resources with others. We should genuinely care that others are able to live well and thrive. So often in the Hebrew Scriptures, the prophets address the failure of the people, as an organized community, to do justice. Their message points to what we are calling *systemic sin*. When the community's structures and systems do harm to those who are vulnerable, it's sin. When the powerholders fail to care for those who are marginalized, it's sin. We miss the mark in relation to God's ideal community revealed and established in Jesus. Prophets remind God's people of their obligation as a society to care for those vulnerable among them. They proclaim that repentance, returning to God, means they need to amend the communal practices that cause these exclusions.

The book of Isaiah provides an example of exactly this sort of prophetic word. In the first section of the book (chapters 1–39), Isaiah is called by God to proclaim that those in power, those who are supposed to care for the vulnerable, are instead getting richer on the backs of those who are poor. They are adding to the burden rather than alleviating it. And their claims to worship God and offer sacrifices as if holy and obedient to God aren't fooling anyone. Especially not God. The prophet announces, "What to me is the multitude of your sacrifices? . . . I have had enough of burnt offerings" (Isa. 1:11). The prophet tells the people to stop pretending they're obedient to God and instead "cease to do evil, learn to do good; seek justice, rescue the oppressed, defend the orphan, plead for the widow" (Isa. 1:17). Lest we assume this points to individuals failing to do as God wills, we then find a clear reference to the concept of systemic sin: "Ah, you who make iniquitous decrees, who write oppressive statutes, to turn aside the needy from justice and to rob the poor of my people of their right" (Isa. 10:1–2). Laws, decrees, communal standards, rules, and regulations that are used to exclude some and privilege others. It's systemic sin.

The source of the problem faced by Judah and Jerusalem is social injustice, perhaps caused by their idolatry or simply their choice to put other gods ahead of the one true God. For our communities today, those gods are money, power, pleasure, self. I often think the height of today's idolatry is the idolatry of the self. Isn't this what social media encourages? How many likes can I get? Am I going viral? How many followers do I have? That last one should make us sit up and take note. Whom are we following really? Thanks to the internet and filter bubbles, we are given exactly the information that confirms what we already believe true. This is confirmation bias at work. The self at the center will never draw near to the reign of God on earth. It's erected too many barriers, statutes, and decrees designed for the powerholders to stay on the pedestal.

Nonetheless, laws do make a valuable contribution to society; we can't live without them. At their best, they allow a community to flourish and increase social capital. But laws that are either unfairly applied or not upheld by the people will lead to injustice. In any case, all of the people are in the situation together, even if it's the powerful who are writing the laws and issuing the decrees that do harm. In the case of God's people in Jerusalem in the time of Isaiah, they would all be conquered. Those who are rich, poor, powerful, vulnerable, old, young, men, women. Those who were privileged would be taken into exile in Babylon. Those vulnerable would be left to fend for themselves amid the ruins. They acted as if they weren't one people. But they rose or fell as a whole.

And while many will claim that God then "punishes" these people with exile, their situation is not unlike when we tell one of our kids, "If you keep running with that crowd, something bad is going to happen." We aren't predicting the future; we're seeing the consequences that arise out of wrong action. So, too, with God's people. The people of Judah ignore social justice and turn away from proper relationships—they refuse to love as God loves—and they fail to provide for the needs of those who are vulnerable, those who really can't help themselves. Worst of all, they decide to make an alliance with Egypt, the place that once held them captive. If you choose to go back to the place of your past captivity, to return to that which diminished your life, it can't end well. You keep running with that crowd, nothing good will come of it. And sure enough, Babylon defeats the people and takes the society's privileged into exile, leaving in the ruins of Jerusalem those who are poor and vulnerable, whom they refused to defend in the first place. The failure of those who were leaders to stay in right relationship with God and others led to their own demise. If you say you love God and neighbor but you don't pursue justice in society, it might just be a good time for a careful reading of Isaiah.

This concern for communal justice extends into the New Testament, finding expression in Jesus. In Luke 4, his first sermon back at his home synagogue places an exclamation point on justice. Jesus opens the scroll to the words of the prophet Isaiah: "The Spirit of the Lord is upon me, because he has anointed me to bring good news to the poor. He has sent me to proclaim release of the captives and recovery of sight to the blind, to let the oppressed go free" (Luke 4:18). Then Jesus rolls up the scroll and says, "'Today this scripture has been fulfilled in your hearing'" (Luke 4:21). Ellen Davis refers to this reading from Isaiah as Jesus's "mission statement from Nazareth."[25] Jesus even goes on to tell the naysayers among those hearers that Elijah, another prophet, was sent as a foreigner to a poor widow woman and her fatherless son in Zarephath, a Phoenician city, so that the three of them might together survive the drought and famine (Luke 4:25–26).[26] What does it suggest that this is where Jesus begins his ministry?

The Greek word in the New Testament that is translated as "righteousness" is *dikaiosune*. It means "the right way of thinking, feeling, and acting" and, in a narrower sense, "justice." It comes from the root word *diakios*, translated in the New Testament (NIV) some forty-one times as "righteous" and thirty-three times as "just."[27] It means "equitable." It suggests that our whole being—spirit, heart, mind, and actions—is aligned with the way of love expressed most fully in Jesus Christ. So when Jesus says, "I have come not to call the *diakios*, but the sinners to repentance" (Luke 5:32), he's announcing that those who are living in radical relationships that uphold life for all, especially the ones who are vulnerable, are not in need of a radical realignment. Rather, those who are missing the mark and not creating and sustaining God-given, life-giving social arrangements need to turn outward from their false constructs and toward God, to listen deeply, to take on the mind of Christ, and to live in a way that expresses our inescapable interrelatedness. Biblical justice is "'social' because it is about relationships."[28] If our human organizations don't match the ideal expressed in God's *basileia* that has drawn near in Jesus, we will miss the mark, and injustice will be present, whether intentional or not.

You can't proclaim that you love everyone but allow systems to do them harm. If we understand that justice requires change in communities—whether our faith community, an international business conglomerate, a government and its laws, or even the global community—then adaptive leadership principles can help us to act more justly, as long as we are practicing the spiritual disciplines we've discussed throughout this book such that our mind might more closely align with that of Christ, who sees and acts perfectly. Even if we don't like what Jesus says or does, he hasn't missed the mark. We just haven't yet grown enough to realize it. We can close our minds to his teachings we don't like, but that won't change them. It just keeps us from aligning with the ideal community established in Jesus.

Adaptive leadership—with its model of reflection, action, feedback, reflection, action, feedback—can apply to the community of faith as it "gets on the balcony" to observe whatever harm a system or organization might be doing. We can then experiment with tangible acts that could result in some changes to the system. We can't "fix" the problem that exists as a broad external context. But we can do our part, especially in addressing the injustice in our own community. Like a prophet, we are called to speak and act in ways that can promote change in an unjust system. And like a prophet, we might not be successful in producing the change God asks us to seek. But our calling to lead with love remains.

Every prophet knows that God's love is too often rejected. The Word of God comes to the people and says: Change your ways! Help others who are poor and vulnerable. Break the church's rules if someone is hungry, and go ahead and glean that wheat on Sunday. Touch someone who is unclean and unworthy according to your standards. Invite that "sinner" to your home for a meal, or better yet, go to their house for all to see. First-century religious leaders (like twenty-first-century religious leaders) had a lot of rules they considered essential to "holiness" or "godliness." They excluded those they considered "sinful" and made them unworthy of God. Maybe they had acne (read Leviticus 13 if you don't understand this point). Maybe they were menstruating. Maybe they migrated from a foreign land. Maybe they had a disability. The religious leaders explained human conditions that they didn't understand as being caused by personal sin. But their systemic sin was the real problem. I think when Jesus says, "Go and sin no more," he's trying to tell someone they are worthy of God and life. He's saying: Don't internalize the message that you're sinful just because someone tells you so. You are loved. You are fearfully and wonderfully made. If you're missing the mark, adjust. If you're being told you're unworthy, I say you're loved.

Hopefully, we've learned something over the past two thousand years and have been informed by the miracles and wonders of science. Today, so many of those conditions called "sinful" in the Bible have scientific explanations. Even a hurricane or tornado can be explained apart from being an "act of God," despite those stage-one preachers who claim it's God's punishment—but only if the tragedy happens in a place they've already judged to be ungodly and unworthy. The most destructive and pervasive sin exists through systems and structures created by human beings. We are our own worst enemies. Without seeking justice, we cannot lead with love. Cease to do evil. Learn to do good. Seek justice. This is the way of love.

And so we arrive at the meaning and power of the resurrection. Resurrection requires change. Resurrection means some things have to die so that new life might emerge in us and in our world. And, yes, the faith community, as the body of Christ, is subject to this pattern. As Michael Plekon writes, "Death and resurrection define the community that follows Jesus. . . . for the body of Christ is always at once crucified, dying and raised, a new life."[29] In fact, Plekon identifies multiple ways faith communities are experiencing resurrection through experiments or "efforts to reinvent, repurpose, and restructure themselves."[30] Reforming society often means reforming ourselves. Unless we change in ways that promote love and justice for all, we'll never find new life, resurrection, healing, and wholeness. Resurrection can and does happen, even in a time of church decline. Leading with love in the midst of change and loss can and does bring new life into our faith community and our world. Leading with justice changes the world one step at a time. The Word still becomes flesh in time, space, and circumstances. Let the Word become flesh in your context.

Practice Makes (More but Not Completely) Perfect

1. Do a SWOT or SCOPE analysis. Then discuss with your leadership team what the full picture suggests for leading your faith community toward God's future.
2. When you map the internal, external immediate, and broad external contexts, where are you being led by the Spirit to move in new directions? Where are you missing the mark? How might you better embody the reign of God that has drawn near in Jesus?
3. Take your faith community's vitals and get some sense of your spiritual health.
4. How do you understand the prophetic call as a part of Jesus's own ministry in the world? Do you feel comfortable in leading prophetic ministry? Does your faith community see justice as central to the love of God in our world?

Resources for Going Deeper

Ammerman, Nancy T., Jackson W. Carroll, Carl S. Dudley, and William McKinney, eds. *Studying Congregations: A New Handbook*. Nashville: Abingdon, 1998.

Bolsinger, Tod. *Canoeing the Mountains: Christian Leadership in Uncharted Territory*. Downers Grove, IL: IVP, 2015.

Heifetz, Ronald, Alexander Grashow, and Marty Linsky. *The Practice of Adaptive Leadership: Tools and Tactics for Changing Your Organization and the World*. Boston: Harvard Business Press, 2009.

Heifetz, Ronald, and Marty Linsky. *Leadership on the Line: Staying Alive through the Dangers of Change*. Boston: Harvard Business Review Books, 2017.

Keller, Tim. *Generous Justice: How God's Grace Makes Us Just*. New York: Penguin, 2010.

Plekon, Michael. *Community as Church, Church as Community*. Eugene, OR: Cascade Books, 2021.

Conclusion

THE LAST WORD IS ALWAYS *LOVE*

I NEED TO begin this conclusion with an honest confession. I've given a lot of examples in this book of moments when I might have led well. But here's the truth: I'm not a perfect pastor. Not even close. My current faith community, the Village, has a long way to go to restore vitality and long-term sustainability. At times, I'm not sure we can get there. Maybe another pastor would be more successful. But I'm the one asked to lead at such a time as this. The one thing that's clear to me is that the Villagers know I love God and I love them just as they are, with their different ways of seeing and experiencing the world. And I'm pretty sure they love God and others as best they can. We don't argue or fight or nitpick, even though we really do have different perspectives—politically, generationally, theologically—among us. I can't take credit for the love among us, though I try my best to make it our priority. But love is visible in the "fruit" of this faith community.

Love is the gospel of Jesus Christ. It's the gospel stated in one word. It's not possible to "fail" if we are leading with love. The human organization I serve might close someday in the future, but it's not my job to "save" the church. My job is to live into and out of the Great Commandment. My calling is to love God and love people (inside and outside the faith community) and to lead them to do the same. Maybe you relate to this confession. If so, Pastor, take a deep breath. Settle into the Spirit. Listen to God. "All things work together for good, for those who love God" (Rom. 8:28). Among all the stresses of leading a faith community and all the overwhelming problems in our world, there is only one thing that matters. We are called to lead with love. Remember, God is love. If we are putting God first, at the center, and above all else, then love is everything. Without love, we simply are not the body of Christ in the world.

Conforming Our Story to Jesus's Story

When we study and take to heart the life of Jesus, as revealed to us in the Gospels, we consider him the ultimate model for leading with love. Jesus's leadership begins in the form of a helpless, vulnerable baby in need of community to stay alive and thrive. The incarnation demonstrates that we are called to love unconditionally, just as the infant loves infinitely and unconditionally. No biases. No judgment. No pointing out someone's unworthiness. No one is excluded from the view of the manger. Not kings or shepherds. Not animals. Not men or women. Not Jews or gentiles. The manger is a place open to everyone and everything. It reveals the radical relationships that God has already put in place. God's first Word in Jesus is *love*.

But once the child begins to grow, it has to learn and develop in every sense. Jesus wasn't sent into the world as a fully formed human being. Rather, he was exactly like any human being whose brain and body had to grow and learn over time. We are called to the same, as individuals and as human beings. There is never a point when we stop learning if we hope to deepen our love by taking on the mind of Christ. There is so much to learn. How little we know about the created world, but century by century, we discover more that reveals the creative genius of the living God. How little we know about ourselves and our communal formation. But brain science is showing us we need emotional intelligence, an awareness of human bias, insight into cultural difference, and the capacity to analyze contexts. God has created us with brains, just like Jesus, to be able to do these things. When we grow in love, we let go of our defensiveness, the need to be right or holier. Learning these new pastoral skills helps us to let go of the sin of comparisons and to love everyone and everything.

Once we can check that judgment at the door of our encounters with other people, we're on our way to seeing as God sees: not in terms of *this* or *that* but this *and* that. Arriving at the divine *And* is central to the journey of faith, hope, and love. The Great *And* is central to leading with love. Maybe we sense we have no clear path forward as a faith community, *and* by faith we'll set out in a direction, trusting the Spirit will lead and guide us. We see the horrific suffering across the globe and at our doorstep with an immediacy never before possible in human life. The world is overwhelming;

the evil is real. We see the conflict, divisions, disillusionment, decline. *And* we hold to the promises of God, trusting that the world never has the last word. We see so many mass shootings and people dying from floods, fires, hurricanes, and droughts. *And* God will wipe every tear, restore the goodness of creation, reconcile all things, and bring flourishing and the fullness of life to everyone and everything. We see the hatred and dehumanization constructed by human beings and systems that are upheld as "the way things are." *And* we hold fast to God's love poured out in the world as the most powerful, unquenchable force in the universe. Love allows us to speak and act for change and justice.

When faith, hope, and love are the primary qualities of our faith community, then we step out from the walls of our building into a world where Jesus is already among those in need. As the incarnate body of Christ, we must engage in the ministry of Jesus in the world: We heal, we feed, we visit those who are sick and those in prison; we bring life abundantly. We "cease to do evil, learn to do good; seek justice, rescue the oppressed, defend the orphan, plead for the widow" (Isa. 1:16–17). We baptize in the name of the Father, Son, and Holy Spirit (Matt. 28:19)—inviting others into radical, life-giving relationships of love, which is the very nature of the Trinity. We live in mutuality, not power over others. We help them to become learners of Jesus Christ, and they help us to learn. Together, in community, we grow and learn. We teach them to love and to give and discover that they do the same, in their own language, and we understand. We work together to turn hearts outward toward God and each other. We are changed, as at Pentecost, by all nations, tribes, and peoples learning and growing together in Jesus's way of encountering others with love.

But the life of Jesus brings us face to face with another hard reality. Bringing people together doesn't always lead to love. Sharing the way of Jesus with its offer of healing and wholeness is often rejected, even by those who have been baptized. We see the "weeds of the world" sprouting in churches. Division, factions, finger-pointing. Not everyone will choose the way of love. Many will continue in dualistic mindsets that demand that their own way be upheld, and yes, often in the name of God. A faith community, just like an individual, is known by its fruit. As Paul says, "God is not mocked, for you reap whatever you sow" (Gal. 6:7). So we choose to love in the face of those who hate. We love in the face of those who tear down. We love in the face of those who destroy. We love in the face of those who insist on the status quo, despite the harm it's doing. We love even as we are wounded by the transgressions of others. The cross remains as a symbol of reconciliation and a message of love. There will be plenty of people who reject love, often in the name of power, judgment, self-interest, and fear. But we don't respond in kind. We just hang with Jesus, no matter how others might reject our message or accuse us of heresy. The way, the truth, and the life of Jesus is always about bringing people together into relationship. Those who love don't participate in dividing and dealing death to others.

But thanks be to God, the story doesn't end with the cross. Out of the destructiveness of human hearts and systems turned in on themselves— hearts and systems that insist on the sin of comparisons to dehumanize and reject the "other"—God brings new life. God overcomes the world and its weeds. God's love rises to life among us. God's love announces, "Peace be with you." *Shalom*, healing and wholeness. In the midst of a divided world filled with judgment and loss, decline and destruction, God points us to the future where healing and wholeness walk among us in the cool of the evening. Resurrected life comes only when the human body lets go of its need to be right, to be holier, to be better, and to be the one who sets the terms and demands its own way. We are the ones who must change. We are the ones who must stop crucifying the love God poured into the world. We are the ones who haven't yet learned what Jesus is teaching us. But if we learn to listen, God's Spirit will show us and lead us. We will find the depths of life in God. We will find new life, resurrected life. We'll take on the mind of Christ that brings everything together.

So we return to the one thing we can't ignore or set aside: deep listening. *Sola Spiritus*. Spirit alone. Alone with the Spirit. Our hearts yearn for something more. But we don't listen very well to Jesus's teachings, let alone the Spirit. Our ears are filled with a noisy world that demands our attention. Our hearts are so often turned inward that we can only hear the incessant chattering of our own minds. But if we discipline ourselves to seek the Spirit, we will hear and turn outward. We'll learn. We'll take on the mind of Christ. We'll love. Leaders are no different than the people we lead in this process of faith, hope, and love. Yes, there are a million reasons not to place ourselves quietly before God, not to set aside our thinking and feeling and to-do lists: I can't because I have too much to do. Because my house is too noisy. Because I have ADHD. Because I'm too tired. Because. But God won't heal us, won't change us, won't fill us with love without our intentional commitment to the relationship.

The only thing that matters in this life is "faith working through love" (Gal. 5:6). This is our calling in Jesus Christ. It's everyone's calling in Jesus Christ. When we open ourselves to be changed by the Spirit, love will grow in us and among us. When we are attentive to the Spirit, love will find us and take root. When we learn to love first, we'll sow and cultivate "joy, peace, patience, kindness, generosity, faithfulness, gentleness, and self-control" (Gal. 5:22). We'll "pray without ceasing" (1 Thess. 5:17), bringing mindfulness or the mind of Christ to all our interactions with others. The mind of Christ enables us to see and love as God sees and loves. And it begins with simply placing ourselves before the Mystery of the universe and letting go.

Each chapter of this book has offered a summarizing principle that can point us toward leading with love. As leaders, we know we need new skills for ministry. But there is so much to learn that it might seem overwhelming. So start simply. Start by putting in place the contemplative practice that will sustain you throughout your ministry and keep love alive within you. Once you've made that spiritual practice a priority, then gradually work on the other leadership principles. Wherever we begin our work, love will be strengthened in us and in our faith community.

Those of us who lead aren't perfect. We know we'll make mistakes. Sometimes we feel inadequate for the challenges we face. Sometimes we'll simply want to give in to the status quo. Sometimes we'll be tired, stressed, or frustrated. Sometimes we will judge others or ourselves too harshly. We aren't immune to the human condition. But love can become our calling card in the world. When our ministry comes to an end, the only thing that will matter is how well we have loved. Lead with love, for love is the power of healing and wholeness, the power of radical relationship, the power of justice, the power of God. Love always has the final word.

The Six Principles for Leading with Love

Leadership Principle One: Leadership is all about love.
Leadership Principle Two: We are designed to grow, learn, and change.
Leadership Principle Three: Stay open to the Spirit and listen deeply.
Leadership Principle Four: Learn to love yourself so you can love others.
Leadership Principle Five: Learn to see through your neighbor's eyes.
Leadership Principle Six: Let the Word become flesh in your context.

NOTES

Introduction

1 See, notably, Phyllis Tickle, *The Great Emergence: How Christianity Is Changing and Why* (2008; repr., Grand Rapids, MI: Baker Books, 2012).

2 These four characteristics are central to the leadership model presented by Lovett H. Weems Jr., *Church Leadership*, rev. ed. (Nashville: Abingdon, 2010).

3 Roger Heuser and Norman Shawchuck emphasize these skills. *Leading the Congregation: Caring for Yourself While Serving the People*, rev. ed. (Nashville: Abingdon, 2010).

4 Many leadership books today address adaptive change and the process for pursuing it in congregations. See, for example, Tod Bolsinger, *Canoeing the Mountains* (Downers Grove, IL: IVP, 2015); Scott Cormode, *The Innovative Church* (Grand Rapids, MI: Baker Academic, 2020); and Tony Morgan, *The Unstuck Church* (Nashville: Thomas Nelson, 2017).

5 Jacqui Lewis, *Fierce Love* (New York: Harmony Books, 2021), 109.

6 Thomas Jay Oord, *Pluriform Love* (Grassmere, ID: SacraSage Press, 2022), 28.

7 Oord, *Pluriform Love*, 30.

8 Roberta C. Bondi, *To Love as God Loves: Conversations with the Early Church* (Philadelphia: Fortress, 1987), 17.

9 Bondi, *To Love as God Loves*, 20.

10 Bondi, *To Love as God Loves*, 21.

11 Bondi, *To Love as God Loves*, 23.

12 Bondi, *To Love as God Loves*, 27.

13 Throughout this book, I will use the language of *faith communities* as a way of distinguishing those places of spiritual depth and love from *church* as a human institution intent on perpetuating its own standards of life together that may or may not reflect the depths of love in Jesus Christ.

14 Peter G. Northouse, *Leadership: Theory and Practice*, 9th ed. (Thousand Oaks, CA: Sage Publications, 2022), 2.

15 Northouse, *Leadership*, 6.

16 Weems, *Church Leadership*, xv.

17 Weems, *Church Leadership*, 1.

18 Heuser and Shawchuck, *Leading the Congregation*, 13.

19 Carole Becker, *Leading Women* (Abingdon, VA: Nashville, 1996), 23, as cited in Heuser and Shawchuck, *Leading the Congregation*, 12.

20 I've made this claim in my book Elaine Robinson, *These Three: The Theological Virtues of Faith, Hope, and Love* (Cleveland: Pilgrim Press, 2004), 22. I once had an obstetrician tell me an umbilical cord does, indeed, have three intertwined vessels.

21 Richard Rohr, *The Universal Christ: How a Forgotten Reality Can Change the Way We See, Hope for, and Believe* (New York: Convergent Books, 2019), 14.

22 Frank Viola and George Barna, *Pagan Christianity?* (Carol Stream, IL: Barna, 2012), 191.

23 All quotations of Scripture are from the New Revised Standard Version unless otherwise noted.

24 Bruce D. Perry and Oprah Winfrey, *What Happened to You? Conversations on Trauma, Resilience, and Healing* (New York: Flatiron Books, 2021).

25 Often we misunderstand the Ten Commandments. They are the ethical code of Israel that suggests how best to live with God and others so that all might flourish. They point to the love of God and neighbor. The law arises from the practicalities and uncertainties of applying that moral or ethical code in particular circumstances. We should resist the desire to equate the Ten Commandments with our human laws, which vary over time.

1. Growing

1 Joseph A. Fitzmyer, *First Corinthians*, The Anchor Yale Bible Series, vol. 32 (New Haven, CT: Yale University Press, 2008), 52.

2 As Frank Sinatra proclaimed in "New York, New York."

3 Fitzmyer, *First Corinthians*, 474.

4 Fitzmyer, *First Corinthians*, 183.

5 Fitzmyer, *First Corinthians*, 184.

6 Fitzmyer, *First Corinthians*, 488.

7 Fitzmyer, *First Corinthians*, 488.

8 Fitzmyer, *First Corinthians*, 497.

9 Bill Bryson, *The Body: A Guide for Occupants* (New York: Anchor Books, 2021), 48.

10 Bryson, *The Body*, 49.

11 Bryson, *The Body*, 49.

12 Bryson, *The Body*, 50.

13 Bryan, *The Body*, 54.

14 *The Message*, trans. Eugene H. Peterson (Colorado Springs, CO: Nav-Press, 2002).

15 Bryson, *The Body*, 55.

16 Not only does our consciousness or meaning-making change but the human brain itself has changed. Over millennia, the human brain has become smaller. Every human brain, as if by agreement or in the mystery of God, is smaller than our ancestors' brains by about the size of a tennis ball. Bryson, *The Body*, 70. Everything changes. Sometimes growth means less.

17 Here we draw loosely on the framework and analysis of Ken Wilber in *Integral Spirituality: A Startling New Role for Religion in the Modern and Postmodern World* (Boulder, CO: Integral Books, 2006).

18 Nicholas Carr, *The Shallows: What the Internet Is Doing to Our Brains* (New York: W. W. Norton, 2010).

19 For a deeper analysis of myths, see, for example, Joseph Campbell, *Myths to Live By* (New York: Penguin, 1972) or C. G. Jung as analyzed in *Jung on Mythology*, selected and introduced by Robert A. Segal (Princeton, NJ: Princeton University Press, 1998).

20 Louis K. Dupré, *The Enlightenment and the Intellectual Foundations of Modern Culture* (New Haven, CT: Yale University Press, 2004), 7.

21 Here we could point to the homogeneous unit principle (HUP) as characteristic of the modern mindset. This principle of the church growth movement suggests that churches grow best when congregants share similar basic characteristics such as race and ethnicity or socioeconomic status. The church is thus comprised of those who are "like me." More about the HUP in chapter 4.

22 For example, the Tuskegee syphilis experiments or the HeLa cancer cells, taken unknowingly from Henrietta Lacks, which became one of the most important, ongoing sources of medical research.

23 Here we might consider W. E. B. DuBois's notion of *double consciousness*, in which an African American would traverse public spaces through white lenses or norms while living out of black lenses and norms beyond the control of white institutions. For this reason, the black Church was the sole institutional location in the United States (alongside the family) for African American self-determination. It provided a safe place to organize the community to resist white norms and expectations. With

the advent of cell phone videos, white Americans have begun to see, in part, what it is like to be black in the United States.

24 On the exponential rate of technological change, see, for example, Ray Kurzweil, *The Age of Spiritual Machines* (New York: Penguin, 1999). One needn't accept his conclusions about the future of technology in relationship to human life to appreciate his explanation of how rapidly human life has changed and is still changing with our technological advances. Ten years ago, how many faith communities even discussed having a service *livestreamed?*

25 Brian McLaren, *Faith after Doubt: Why Your Beliefs Stopped Working and What to Do about It* (New York: St. Martin's, 2021), 45.

26 McLaren, *Faith after Doubt*, 49.

27 McLaren, *Faith after Doubt*, 64.

28 McLaren, *Faith after Doubt*, 65–66.

29 McLaren, *Faith after Doubt*, 72.

30 McLaren, *Faith after Doubt*, 94.

31 McLaren, *Faith after Doubt*, 97.

32 See Richard Rohr, *Everything Belongs: The Gift of Contemplative Prayer* (New York: Crossroad Publishing, 2003).

33 McLaren, *Faith after Doubt*, 101.

2. Deep Listening

1 Hopefully, we human beings have since learned something that suggests maybe killing other religious leaders isn't such a good idea, even in the name of God.

2 Barbara Brown Taylor, *An Altar in the World* (New York: HarperOne, 2009), xv.

3 Taylor, *An Altar in the World*, xvi.

4 Ronald Rolheiser, *The Holy Longing: The Search for a Christian Spirituality* (New York: Doubleday, 1999), 6.

5 Rolheiser, *The Holy Longing*, 7.

6 Rolheiser, *The Holy Longing*, 11.

7 Marjorie J. Thompson, *Soul Feast: An Invitation to the Christian Spiritual Life*, newly rev. ed. (Louisville, KY: Westminster John Knox Press, 2014), 7.

8 Rohr, *Everything Belongs*, 30.

9 Thomas Keating, *Open Mind, Open Heart* (New York: Continuum, 1997), 93.

10 Keating, *Open Mind, Open Heart*, 101.

11 Ronald Rolheiser, "Contemplative Prayer," ronrolheiser.com (October 10, 2016), https://ronrolheiser.com/contemplative-prayer-2/#.Y0v7 PnbMI2w (accessed October 16, 2022).

12 Henri Nouwen, *The Way of the Heart*, First Ballantine Trade Paperback Edition: December 2003 (New York: Ballantine Books, 1981), 10.

13 Nouwen, *The Way of the Heart*, 36.

14 Nouwen, *The Way of the Heart*, 48.

15 Nouwen, *The Way of the Heart*, 50.

16 Nouwen, *The Way of the Heart*, 50.

17 Keating, *Open Mind, Open Heart*, 11.

18 Keating, *Open Mind, Open Heart*, 11.

19 Nouwen, *The Way of the Heart*, 76. Emphasis mine.

20 Nouwen, *The Way of the Heart*, 76.

21 Keating, *Open Mind, Open Heart*, 15.

22 Keating, *Open Mind, Open Heart*, 15.

23 Thelma Hall, *Too Deep for Words: Rediscovering Lectio Divina* (New York: Paulist Press, 1988). The practice has four steps: 1) reading and listening to a passage of Scripture, 2) reflecting on the passage in one's mind, 3) meditating on the passage within one's heart, and 4) contemplating, in which our thinking, feeling, and knowing cease.

24 Ellen J. Langer, *Mindfulness* (Cambridge, MA: Perseus Books, 1989), 63.

25 Langer, *Mindfulness*, 3.

26 Langer, *Mindfulness*, 19.

27 Langer, *Mindfulness*, 21.

28 Langer, *Mindfulness*, 40.

29 Langer, *Mindfulness*, 64.

30 Langer, *Mindfulness*, 65.

31 Langer, *Mindfulness*, 66–75.

3. Caring

1 Bruce D. Perry and Oprah Winfrey, *What Happened to You? Conversations on Trauma, Resilience, and Healing* (New York: Flatiron Books, 2021), 126–131.

2 Brian McLaren, *Why Don't They Get It? Overcoming Bias in Others (and Yourself)* (e-book, available at www.brianmclaren.net/store/, 2019), 57.

3 McLaren, *Why Don't They Get It?*, 122.

4 Ken Wilber, *Integral Spirituality: A Startling New Role for Religion in the Modern and Postmodern World* (Boulder, CO: Integral Books, 2006).

5 See Wilber, *Integral Spirituality,* 21, for the four-quadrants model. You can use a search engine to find the model online and can also access a free course at https://integrallife.com/build-your-integral-life.

6 For an accessible discussion of the brain science discussed here, see Perry and Winfrey, *What Happened to You?*

7 See David Robson, "There Really Are 50 Eskimo Words for 'Snow,'" *Washington Post* (January 14, 2013), https://www.washingtonpost.com /national/health-science/there-really-are-50-eskimo-words-for-snow /2013/01/14/e0e3f4e0-59a0-11e2-beee-6e38f5215402_story.html (accessed October 26, 2022). For nearly a century, this claim was debated, but now it's generally accepted as true. Another indication that human beings grow and learn over time.

8 See Perry and Winfrey, *What Happened to You?*, 126–132, for an extended discussion of generational trauma.

9 Bryson, *The Body*, 5.

10 Bryson, *The Body*, 5.

11 Bryson, *The Body*, 5.

12 Bryson, *The Body*, 21.

13 Bryson, *The Body*, 7.

14 Bryson, *The Body*, 212.

15 Bryson, *The Body*, 212.

16 Sallie McFague, *The Body of God* (Minneapolis: Fortress Press, 1993), 14–15. McFague reconstructs this dualism into an organic, relational understanding of the material and spiritual.

17 Jim Wilder and Michel Hendriks, *The Other Half of Church: Christian Community, Brain Science, and Overcoming Spiritual Stagnation* (Chicago: Moody Publishers, 2020).

18 Wilder and Hendriks, *The Other Half of Church*, 189.

19 Wilder and Hendriks, *The Other Half of Church*, 45.

20 See, for example, Will Roscoe, *Changing Ones: Third and Fourth Genders in Native North America* (New York: Palgrave Macmillan, 2000).

21 Mirabai Starr, *Wild Mercy: Living the Fierce and Tender Wisdom of the Women Mystics* (Boulder, CO: Sounds True, 2019), 139.

22 Starr, *Wild Mercy*, 139–140.

23 Starr, *Wild Mercy*, 140.

24 This notion that the sacraments reconcile creation, as well as human beings, with God can be found in Dietrich Bonhoeffer, *Christ the Center* (San Francisco: Harper and Row, 1978).

25 Starr, *Wild Mercy*, 67.

26 Starr, *Wild Mercy*, 84.

27 Starr, *Wild Mercy*, 89.

28 Starr, *Wild Mercy*, 138.

29 Richard Rohr, "Contemplation and Right Action," in *Richard Rohr's Daily Meditation* (Albuquerque, NM: Center for Action and Contemplation, August 22, 2022).

30 Benjamin L. Webb and Kristie Chase, "Occupational Distress and Health among a Sample of Christian Clergy," *Pastoral Psychology* 68 (2019): 352. https//doi.org/10.1007/s11089-018-0844-y.

31 Webb and Chase, "Occupational Distress and Health," 335. Studies also show that while physical health declines with age, mental health often improves.

32 Webb and Chase, "Occupational Distress and Health," 340.

33 Webb and Chase, "Occupational Distress and Health," 352.

34 Webb and Chase, "Occupational Distress and Health," 352.

35 Perry and Winfrey, *What Happened to You?*, 142.

36 Perry and Winfrey, *What Happened to You?*, 142.

37 Perry and Winfrey, *What Happened to You?*, 142.

38 David Kinnaman and Mark Matlock, *Faith for Exiles: Five Ways for a New Generation to Follow Jesus in Digital Babylon* (Grand Rapids, MI: Baker Books, 2019), 113.

39 Daniel Goleman, *Emotional Intelligence: Why It Can Matter More than IQ* (New York: Bantam Books, 1995, and a new introduction, 2020), xiii.

40 Goleman, *Emotional Intelligence*, 72.

41 Goleman, *Emotional Intelligence*, 51.

42 Goleman, *Emotional Intelligence*, 170.

43 Perry and Winfrey, *What Happened to You?*, 164.

44 Goleman, *Emotional Intelligence*, 12–13.

45 Perry and Winfrey, *What Happened to You?*, 170.

4. Connecting

1 Perry and Winfrey, *What Happened to You?*, 231.

2 Perry and Winfrey, *What Happened to You?*, 232.

3 Perry and Winfrey, *What Happened to You?*, 234.

4 Jessica Nordell, *The End of Bias: A Beginning* (New York: Metropolitan Books, 2021), 45.

5 Nordell, *The End of Bias*, 48.

6 Nordell, *The End of Bias*, 60.

7 Nordell, *The End of Bias*, 98.

8 Nordell, *The End of Bias*, 64.

9   Nordell, *The End of Bias*, 139.

10   Perry and Winfrey, *What Happened to You?*, 236.

11   Nordell, *The End of Bias*, 95.

12   Nordell, *The End of Bias*, 97.

13   Nordell, *The End of Bias*, 125–126.

14   Perry and Winfrey, *What Happened to You?*, 241.

15   Perry and Winfrey, *What Happened to You?*, 241.

16   Nordell, *The End of Bias*, 52.

17   Jennifer L. Eberhardt, *Biased: Uncovering the Hidden Prejudice That Shapes What We See, Think, and Do* (New York: Viking, 2019), 26.

18   See Donald A. McGavran, *Understanding Church Growth* (Grand Rapids, MI: Eerdmans, 1970).

19   I've had students object that the Bible uses categories of darkness and light, as if night is the color black and day is the color white. This argument tends to expose and confirm the strength of their dualistic, culturally constructed categories shaping what they "see."

20   See, for example, Milton J. Bennett, "Becoming Interculturally Competent," in *Toward Multiculturalism: A Reader in Multicultural Education*, 2nd ed., ed. J. Wurzel (Newton, MA: Intercultural Resource Corporation, 2004).

21   See, for example, Mitch Hammer, "The Intercultural Development Inventory: An Approach for Assessing and Building Intercultural Competence," in *Contemporary Leadership and Intercultural Competence*, ed. Michael A. Moodian (Thousand Oaks, CA: Sage, 2009), 203–218.

22   Gary Byers, "The Biblical Cities of Tyre and Sidon." (Associates for Biblical Research: created January 26, 2010), originally published in *Bible and Spade* (Fall 2002). https://biblearchaeology.org/research/divided-kingdom/4180-the-biblical-cities-of-tyre-and-sidon.

23   Kinnaman and Matlock, *Faith for Exiles*, 15.

24   Kinnaman and Matlock, *Faith for Exiles*, 19.

5. Embodying

1   Carl Sandburg, "Four Preludes on Playthings of the Wind," in *The Complete Poems of Carl Sandburg* (New York: Harcourt, Brace, Jovanovich, 1970), 183.

2   Although SWOT analysis is often attributed to Albert Humphrey, its origin is unclear.

3   An excellent resource describing the neighborhood tour and other methods of analysis is *Studying Congregations: A New Handbook*, ed.

Nancy T. Ammerman et al. (Nashville: Abingdon, 1998). The section "Conducting a Space Tour" is found on pages 47–50.

4 Ronald Heifetz, Alexander Grashow, and Marty Linsky, *The Practice of Adaptive Leadership: Tools and Tactics for Changing Your Organization and the World* (Boston: Harvard Business Press, 2009), 14.

5 Heifetz, Grashow, and Linsky, *The Practice of Adaptive Leadership*, 14.

6 The analysis that follows is taken from Kevin Ford's unpublished slides, "Analytics and Insight: From the Transforming Church Insight (Pre-Pandemic)." I am grateful to Kevin for his generosity in sharing this information. Deeper analysis will be provided in his forthcoming book with Jim Singleton, *The Attentive Church* (Downers Grove, IL: InterVarsity Press, forthcoming).

7 Heifetz, Grashow, and Linsky, *The Practice of Adaptive Leadership*, 31.

8 Ronald Heifetz and Marty Linsky, *Leadership on the Line: Staying Alive through the Dangers of Change* (Boston: Harvard Business Review Books, 2017), 107.

9 Heifetz and Linsky, *Leadership on the Line*, 108.

10 Heifetz, Grashow, and Linsky, *The Practice of Adaptive Leadership*, 70.

11 The simplified matrix is found in Heifetz, Grashow, and Linsky, *The Practice of Adaptive Leadership*, 6.

12 Heifetz, Grashow, and Linsky, *The Practice of Adaptive Leadership*, 22.

13 Thomas Jay Oord, *Pluriform Love* (Grassmere, ID: SacraSage Press, 2022), 28.

14 Oord, *Pluriform Love*, 31.

15 Oord, *Pluriform Love*, 31.

16 Ellen F. Davis, *Biblical Prophecy: Perspectives for Christian Theology, Discipleship, and Ministry* (Louisville, KY: Westminster John Knox Press, 2014), 7.

17 Davis, *Biblical Prophecy*, 7.

18 Davis, *Biblical Prophecy*, 7.

19 Davis, *Biblical Prophecy*, 7.

20 Tim Keller, *Generous Justice: How God's Grace Makes Us Just* (New York: Penguin Books, 2010), 1. See also Keller, "What Is Biblical Justice?" *Relevant Magazine* (August 23, 2012), http://relevantmagazine.com/faith/what-biblical-justice/ (accessed September 29, 2022).

21 An understanding of this collective perspective of Indigenous peoples is articulated by Steven Charleston, "Theory—Articulating a Native American Theological Theory," in *Coming Full Circle: Constructing Native Christian Theology*, ed. Steven Charleston and Elaine A. Robinson (Minneapolis: Fortress, 2015), 15–16.

22 A good analysis of social capital and its decline in the United States is Robert Putnam's *Bowling Alone: The Collapse and Revival of American Community*, revised and updated (New York: Simon and Schuster, 2000).

23 Elaine A. Robinson, "Faith, Hope, and Love in an Age of Terror," in *Faith, Hope, Love, and Justice*, ed. Anselm K. Min (Lanham, MD: Lexington Books, 2018), 167.

24 Keller, *Generous Justice*, 10.

25 Davis, *Biblical Prophecy*, 75.

26 The story of Elijah and the widow of Zarephath is from 1 Kings 17.

27 This discussion of Greek words is drawn from Strong's Concordance online at Blue Letter Bible, https://www.blueletterbible.org/lexicon/g1342/rsv/tr/0-1/ (accessed October 5, 2022).

28 Keller, *Generous Justice*, 9.

29 Michael Plekon, *Community as Church, Church as Community* (Eugene, OR: Cascade Books, 2021), 60.

30 Plekon, *Community as Church*, 61.